THE TURNIP TRUCK STOPS HERE

Arlyn Vierkant

PublishAmerica
Baltimore

First printing

ISBN: 1-4241-3483-8
PUBLISHED BY PUBLISHAMERICA, LLLP
www.publishamerica.com
Baltimore

Printed in the United States of America

Dedicated to my lovely wife, Susan, and our six children who kept the carbon burned out of the Old Truck.

ACKNOWLEDGMENTS

The Old Truck wanted to thank the little Ford Ranger down the street and its running buddy, the red S-10, that hangs out with it behind the muffler shop downtown. However, after considerable thought, and some insistence on my part, we decided that this would not be wise.

We do definitely want to thank Silvana Vierkant, my daughter, for her extensive cleaning and polishing of this project. By the way, The Old Truck thinks that her Jeep Liberty is pretty sharp too.

Ok, the Old Truck is starting to mutter that if I am going to recognize people, it should also have the privilege of turning its spotlight on Regina Ranger. So I will close this out with one more group of people: the students at Jacksonville College, the University of Texas at Tyler, Tyler Junior College, and Stephen F. Austin State University, who through the years, challenged my pronouncements, laughed at my stale war stories and who, in many cases, inspired me with their faith in God and their love for their families.

Arlyn Vierkant

FOREWORD

To actually believe that a writer has wisdom or personal information of such magnitude or importance that it should be committed to the written page borders either on inflated egotism or its close cousin, "stupidity." What right does a mere mortal have to believe that he or she possesses insights or understandings that are not already stored in the cobwebbed information banks of others?

A quick hike thorough your local religious or secular bookstore will reveal to your wandering gaze shelf after shelf of moldering vanity. Everyone wants to write a book, either personally or through a ghost (not to be taken in the spiritual sense), in order to etch their thoughts in history. Certainly there are tomes which catch your eye; artistically appealing dust covers, titles which titillate the imagination or even worse the passions, experts claiming that they have the solutions to your deepest and most cherished anguish. Many books contain redundant babblings that merely consume raw materials which should have been left in our disappearing forests. Would it not have been far better if one of these fine trees had fallen on the author's vanity rather than being forced into the state of processed pulpwood?

That being said, why is this particular literary effort being initiated? Is it at the prodding of vanity? I certainly hope not! Chasing after vanity requires too much effort in contrast with the objective to be achieved. Is it because I can, a rationalization that one of our former Presidents used in order to explain away some questionable behavior? No, I have other things to do. Do I crave attention and recognition? Well, we all do to some extent, but recognition attracts superficial people. I don't like superficial people. Is it the desire to acquire riches? Unknown authors have the same chance of becoming wealthy through their writings as the typical multi-marketing hostage has in acquiring his beachfront Florida mansion. Unless you are already rich, famous, or a nice combination thereof, turning out the written word is not going to get you a new Scion B (the object of my covetous nature) or anything else you value in this lifetime. Am I smithing words because I have a particular political or religious cause? Well, this cannot be completely ruled out as we all seem to have some "unconscious" motivations for which we advocate in a robot-like manner. However, after further consideration, it must not be a "cause-driven" exercise that I have embarked upon as I am not a heroic figure nor do I feel that I can change human nature. I have met many individuals who are mentally chained by their idealistic philosophies and I am not one of them. Sure, in my younger days, I too had idealistic notions, most of which were projected upon the failings of others, but I have long progressed beyond that contaminated and contemptible level of thought.

The next possible motivator that I considered was that of responsibility. Perhaps I felt that I should be warning others about the error of their ways. I have at least partially shaken this need with the rather pathetic rationalization that "everyone must choose for himself/herself the path to follow." After all, in our society which is enthralled with situational ethics, there really isn't a common definition of "appropriate" behavior anymore. We are too "advanced" in our civilized experience to worry about norms and values. People living on the brink do not want to be disturbed by commonsense intervention. Those uninhibited by social boundaries sometimes have to hit rock bottom before the significance of the "thou shalt nots" kicks into their awareness.

Ok, the good reasons for not developing a manuscript have been laid out for your evaluation. Now on a more proactive note, I will reveal the real reason that I initiated this effort. One day I realized why I had to finally discipline myself to write this manuscript, with the firm intention that it would not be relegated to the closet floor like many of my other projects. The time was right to confirm that we are indeed living in a time of nonsense and futility. The title of the work would not be Ecclesiastes, but rather "The Turnip Truck Stops Here." It was time to look stupidity in the eye and classify it for what it really is. We are not flowing comfortably through life in some sort of continuous dream-state or, even worse, within a treadmill dream. We are really living among people, some of whom do not have a clue. Rather than being politically and culturally correct, it is time to offer such the benefit of our disagreement, even if it has to take the form of ridicule. It is time to draw a line in the sand (using care as many individuals allow their cats to roam freely in such areas). It is time to turn off the ignition of the old Turnip Truck and unload the parasitical cargo.

How did this revelation take place? Was there a thunderbolt out of the blue? Did I see an image preserved in some mold on an unwashed restroom wall? Was I hit by a supernatural force which knocked me backwards on a stage and caused me to quiver in front of well-placed cameras while a showman appealed to his audience for a portion of their tithe? No, the impulse came in a much more mundane manner. I was standing in a post office line waiting to purchase the correct postage on a package. The line inched slowly, while the postal workers seemed mired in mud. Finally, I was only one patron from my objective, the sacred counter. The fine young lady ahead of me requested postage on a small package to be sent somewhere where the pony express still runs, when the entire situation took a terrible turn. The postal clerk looked wearily at the customer and asked the fatal question, "Do you want this sent first class or for a few cents more it can be sent priority mail?" The customer stiffened, sweat beaded on her forehead and she counter-questioned, "How much more?" The response from the postal clerk, "It will be a few cents more." The customer paled, rubbed the palm of her hand against her skirt and made the admission to the clerk, to the others waiting in line, and to her God, "I don't know." Silence enveloped the lobby, traffic on the street outside seemed to slow, tension soared, we all squirmed in silence…what decision would be made? Just before the clowns danced in, the customer made a battlefield decision. She said to the clerk, "What do you think I should do?" Confidence in human nature began to rise. Patrons began to relax. A decision was about to be made. Then the rafters once again began to tremble as the postal clerk responded, "It's your decision." Just as I was groping in my pocket for a nickel to donate to the cause of justice and to the American Way, the customer rotated one more time and decisively stated, "Oh, let's go with the cheapest way."

The calvary appeared on the horizon, only to witness the clerk prolong the agony by asking the customer if she wanted a return receipt, if she wanted to use her credit card, if she needed stamps, etc. However, the crisis had passed and I was a changed man. I was going to write a book. I had witnessed an event that the world may never witness again. I appreciated the anguish of the poor customer, especially when the clerk looked over her shoulder at the line of patrons eagerly awaiting the drama to play out. Then a feeling of empathy set in. Why did the post office confront Jane Doe with such a terrible decision? This lady might be ruined for the rest of the day, battered by the guilt of her hasty decision. This thought was followed by globalization. Why is our society in such a mess? Why are our institutions so pathetic; whether it be the post office, or the political, economic, educational, family, or other more traditional entities?

It was time to release the handbrake on the old Turnip Truck. It was time to write a book.

CHAPTER I

RELIGION

What finer topic for discussion than religion in our modern world? Of all the parking lots found in our society in which the Turnip Truck is most likely to suffer "dings" from manipulative and uncaring door slams and untended shopping carts, it is in the locale of religious pretense.

I find that the word "religion" has taken on an unfortunate connation in our "enlightened" society. It is used much like the term "spirituality," which carries a rather circular popular definition of being spiritual. It is a continuum word which ranges from observance of some sort of spiritualized form of behavior to something that is overly zealous in some ill-defined belief system or perhaps even having a clinical designation of "religiosity."

To take this discussion one step further, I am not even convinced that I like "religious" people. The term brings up a mental image of someone who acts "holier than thou," or of someone who fits the stereotype of an aggressive, proselytizing preacher with silver hair carefully combed into a ducktail, with gleaming white teeth, and treacherous pig-like eyes. This mental image usually has his right hand pumping yours, while his left hand is groping for your wallet.

I encountered these religious types when my wife and I lived in a small town in Colorado. We made the mistake of visiting several churches in the area, both to get acquainted with the local population and to try to find a comfortable association with fellow-believers. We soon recognized the error of our ways. It was on Tuesday evenings when the marauding religious leaders struck, often making uninvited visits to our home from a couple of churches at the same time. Fortunately, we lived about two miles from town, North of the Arkansas River, from where we could see car lights crossing the bridge. We would douse the lights in the house and would sit huddled silently in our home until the tail lights of the predators crossed the bridge back into town. Have you ever noticed that many preachers are late-risers, possibly so that they can trap the unsuspecting late at night? One evening when the light switch was not tripped quickly enough, a preacher sat talking to us until after midnight. At that point, I stood up, announced that he could visit with my wife as long as they could tolerate each other, but I was a working man and I was going to bed. Yes, my marital vows survived this special moment in our married life, but there was extended discussion about it in the morning (until I interrupted and informed her that I was a working man and had to go to the office). Recently, here in the Lone Star State, I observed a new wrought iron gate and sign erected at the entrance of someone's driveway. I must describe what I saw in full detail as it is something that I highly desire in dealing with uninvited religious people. The sign had four mounted and armed cowboys silhouetted on the top part of the structure with the words, "Go Away" cut out in high relief. The word I would add to my sign would be "Preachers" followed by an asterisk which would warn, "unless you come here to worship God."

Certainly, you protest, this guy really has a hang up with preachers! Not really. I believe that there are many servants of God who have been called to shepherd His flock here on earth, men who work tirelessly, without thought of earthly riches or public praise. It is just that I feel there should be more of these men and fewer of the "career seekers" who wish to establish monuments to themselves. There are several ways to establish an informed opinion about a clergyman. First of all, the observers must be familiar with the guy's textbook and whether he knows and loves what is in it. We should notice whether or not the fellow likes people. Is he wonderful, charismatic, and warm on the platform, but distant and uninvolved with the unwashed masses when not performing? Does he follow the commands and instructions of God or does he place himself, his wife, and his family above the members of his flock, or worse, above his service to God? Would you like to be in a room with him when the Lord returns?

Have you noticed during the past few years that the organizations that seem to have the most money for constructing new edifices are the banks and the churches? When people think they are exaggerating by claiming that their little town has a church on every corner, they may not be that far off base. Now, I am all for such buildings as long as they are erected to the glory of God, or, in the case of banks, to the glory of Mammon. There is something spiritually refreshing about a new chapel with beautiful stained glass windows and a cross or crucifix over a polished wooden altar that even resists diminution by the arrival of the duck-tailed preacher. Too many of our church buildings today are modeled after efficient meeting halls, which psychologically removes the sense of awe and dignity that should be experienced by the worshiper. I have had to get used to entering through the sanctuary doors of such buildings to experience not peace, respect, nor devotion, but rather, loud laughter, conversation, and disruption. Being an "old fogy," I still feel a sense of unreality when I see a "gentleman" entering the church proper without removing his headgear. Probably one of the saddest cases of disrespect that I have observed was an elderly gentleman sitting in a pew prior to the beginning of a service with his head bent in prayer. While this communion with the Lord was taking place, two adult males decided to conduct a loud secular conversation over the worshiper's bowed head, one standing in the pew behind and the other in the pew in front of God's elderly child. Don't you secretly (and with appropriate shame, of course) wish for a lightening bolt at a time like that? I have to watch myself when it comes to the temptation to utter those little impulsive prayers for God to reveal His Justice. Several years ago, I was in attendance at a service in which the pastor was obviously misleading his congregation in some of his sermon comments. My prayer: "Let the little sucker take one step further and fall flat on his face off the stage." God did not honor my prayer that day, because He is gracious and long suffering, even with a sinner such as me.

Then there is the large church that we really like led by a pastor who obviously has been blessed with preaching talent from above. However, when you enter the church to worship God, you have to pass by a fully operational bookstore, with its special sales on merchandise. My wife is getting tired of my repetitious observation, "I wonder if the Lord will show up today with a whip to run off the merchandisers?"

If I ever strike oil in my front yard and the mineral rights are still intact, I am going to build a chapel much like the one that existed at Drake University years ago. It was a small hexagonal building into which worshipers could enter in silence and sit in pews around a large circular granite stone that had God's rays of light beaming through a skylight in an otherwise darkened sanctuary. Unfortunately, many students may not realize what a blessing such a structure can be. How wonderful to contemplate one's relationship with God without some "ducktail" reading the latest internet jokes to you over a million dollar sound system.

In reading at random on the Internet, I came across an article that suggested that one successful "religious" organization sent surveyors into the neighborhoods to determine what residents did not like about churches, doctrine, etc. If this story is accurate, the result was that the new organization deleted those things which were offensive in order to spur numerical growth. This is troubling, as much of our Christian belief system is offensive to the residents of this world. The cross has become an offense to many if not to most. If you take the offense out, how much spiritual wealth do you have left? I do not consider myself to be a stupid person, although as I grow older, I learn how little I do know. However, I cannot conceptualize or understand what it is that is developed or accomplished in a religious organization when you slowly diminish the object of worship and His teachings. Is there really a need for large, religiously-oriented social clubs with their varied support groups? When you leave a church service and have experienced an hour of entertainment, has your spiritual relationship been enhanced? Being somewhat overly critical in my perspective on "entertainment religion," I usually watch the "performer" in the singing group or choir who is wiggling the most. It reminds me of the professional football player who points to the sky after a successful sports moment. I would rather that the wiggler and the athlete be honest and scream, "Here I am, look at me, look at me!" The final touch is often added when the director of the performance gazes blissfully into the theater lights and muses, "The applause is all for you Lord." I must surmise that when the applause meter does not top out for some of the popular renditions, the congregation is praising the Lord less.

My wife and I are members of one of those dreadful "support groups," established by many churches to relieve the "shepherd" of the flock from visitation and from getting truly involved with his "sheep." Unfortunately, members of such groups are often really the wooly creatures in point. Members do not question the reason for the gathering, nor do they really know what they are supposed to accomplish during the gathering. However they do know that they are required to meet monthly. When it came time for our turn to host the group, I suggested to my wife, "Let's eat (you always eat before one of these things) and then let's pose the question, "Who/What is God?" Somehow, God does not seem to be very real in either our everyday work lives or in these artificial, scripted "church" meetings. I have to wonder, if the Lord walked in (I know this is bad theology, but play along with me to make a point), would we remove the eggplant from our mouths and greet Him with a booming "Good Morning"? This salutation seems to be a necessary ritual for many pastors in order to crank up a worship service. It appears that this "salute thing" is a technique which is supposed to bond the preacher with his congregation. If the technique is followed to its illogical climax, it is followed by a "group hug," or, if you are lucky, a handshake with a coached statement such as "You sure look fine, little lady!" The truck just backfired, which indicates that I am starting to spin out of control in my comments and had better get back on track!

I recently opined to a college class that it was my humble opinion that less than 10 percent of active church members truly believe in a real, powerful, just God. This comment, of course, aroused some of the sleepers who could hardly picture themselves prone on the floor in the presence of an angry Judge. In reality, a true believer would most certainly be face down among the cigarette butts on the floor, quivering in fear and awe from being in the Holy Presence. Of course, if we as believers would be totally overcome by the majesty and power of God, just think about what this presence would do to the nonbeliever who finally was brought face to face with the ultimate reality in his life. What am I saying? Church people, religious people, whatever we want to call them, are pretty nonchalant about their worship practices. Christ the Friend is still part of the Godhead, last time I checked anyway, but He also is part of the Holy Trinity with God the Judge. I would also wager that the duck-tailed preacher hiding as best he could behind his transparent pulpit, if he really believed, would have to hit the deck also. He most certainly would do so even if he did not believe because it would be difficult to deny the Reality before him. Wouldn't it be wonderful to watch this confrontation? Of course, we probably would not be able to see it because our own noses would be pushed two inches into the floor. I wonder whether those two men loudly talking over the praying white head would be doing the same were Christ to be sitting in the pew with the elderly gentleman praying for us? I suspect that if they were able, they would be.

Enough for titillating digression. We are on a serious topic here. Let's get down to the positive side of this morass of meandering thought. If we really do not like what we are finding in our churches and among "professed" Christians today, is there anything that we should like? Is there anything we can do about it? A big resounding "yes" here! (Ducktail would have the advantage of a drumroll at this point, so, if you would like, just thump the book a few times to get your perspective greased up and ready to go. The Old Truck still has several cans of the really good stuff that it loves to have forced through his zerk fittings. Greasing of a perspective is always good.)

First of all, we should like the fact that there are a number of dedicated believers left in our world. They just might not be found in the expected places. For example, some of them are not members of an organized church, but do strive to assemble with other believers on a more informal basis. Some may not even have that privilege. Some of them are students in secular colleges or kids who could not afford to attend private "Christian Schools." It always deeply touches me when I grade a paper from a college student who manages to work in a brief reference to the reality of his faith. When this is written in a state university setting, it takes on an even larger dimension.

A few of these believers are actually ordained pastors. What sets them apart is that they obviously were called to the field by the Lord rather than merely by a religious organization. They freely give of themselves, often work full time at a non-church related job in order to support their families, yet find time to visit, exhort, teach, and support. How different these are from some of our church leaders who seem to feel that their "professional" staff almost has to equal the number of souls on their carefully updated counts. Hint: When you are visiting a church, swivel your head a few times and see if you can spot the "bean counters" who are carefully recording numbers when their total concentration should be on the object of our worship. Oh, I forgot, that object is not clearly defined in many of the highly structured organizations. In fact, if I understand early church history correctly, the church (read "believers") met together in small clusters in private homes. Denominations did not arise until the wise and arrogant (read "religious leaders") dipped their oar into the puddle of veneration and made it into an ocean of confusion spiced by conflict. It is not size of the worship palace, number of people in attendance, or even limo service to and from the parking lots that truly matters, but rather, it is the day to day striving for obedience and the effort to glorify our Lord God that should be the reason for our continued existence. Remember, this group of believers may be smaller than one would wish, but the individuals are still with us. Wouldn't it be nice if every true believer would be required to dye his or her hair green so we could have the benefit of mutual recognition. No, on second thought, this is not such a good idea. I believe I just heard the old Turnip Truck grind its brakes at the former suggestion.

A former dorm mate of mine was about to enter seminary and since he did not seem to have an identified calling to the field, I wondered what his motivation could be to follow a rather demanding educational preparation which would not usually return good financial rewards. His answer was very direct and only contained a little levity, "It's the women, the seminarians always attract the best looking girls." He went on to marry a beautiful young lady. I liked this young man. Unlike many religious professionals, he had good self-awareness and only a little duplicity.

What else is there to like about today's religious environment? Well, I think it is pretty evident that God has not given up on us yet. Regardless of whether or not you believe that scripture supports the concept of an actual rapture of believers and regardless of how you interpret the millennial dispensations, it is evident that the Holy Spirit is active in us, around us, and through us. God answers prayer. Sure, it is in His own time and according to His Will, but most of us have experienced His Divine Presence. It may be in the most ridiculous minor situations, but things happen that cannot be accounted for by chance or coincidence. I unashamedly pray about everything, especially those things which go badly for me. It sometimes makes me wonder why God tolerates my whining and sudden appearance when I am upset. Certainly, the King of the Universe has other things to be concerned about than little things that go wrong for one of the least of his followers. But, hey, if God is willing, who am I not to turn to Him?

I have prayed about little things and "coincidentally" everything worked out as if there were an answer from God. One of the first things that comes to mind was when I lost my wallet several years ago. The few dollars contained did not bother me so much as the loss of my credit card, insurance cards, and other random notes on torn edges of newspaper that I habitually squirrel in the pockets of my billfold. I searched all through the house, I tore the car up, I retraced my steps, I intellectually considered all the possibilities of where it could have dropped with no results. Then in desperation I turned to God with the simple request, "God, please let me find that wallet." I went through the house one more time and as I walked through the laundry room, for some reason, my glance was drawn to the lint wastebasket that my wife keeps on the floor next to the dryer. There, partially covered with lint, was my wallet. Yes, I thanked God, even though my human side had the thought bouncing through my mind, "How did it get in there?" I know, I know…you must have had more significant prayers answered, but, as this is my book, I am going to share my experiences.

Yet another experience also really had me sweating. (It is ok to sweat if you are worried when you are a guy……women glisten) It occurred one day while I was walking across the grounds of a large institution at which I once worked, with what we referred to as the "great-grandmaster key" on a leather strap. Urban legend had it that if anyone lost this key, they would be financially responsible for re-keying all the ward doors in this large psychiatric institution to which it belonged. I sat down at my desk, tossed my keys in a drawer and noticed to my horror that the "Key" was missing. I immediately retraced my steps across campus, searching the grounds for the missing key, while at the same time glancing at mental patients milling around the area that I had just crossed. This was bad. Imagine a paranoid patient walking around the grounds at night randomly opening locked doors. Completing the circuit, I sat down at my desk and was about to call security and make my desperate confession. In my anguish, I prayed to God, "Once more, help this old loser out?" I then retraced my steps the approximate three city blocks that I had walked, when a reflection on metal drew my attention. There lying in the grass, not more than a few yards from where patients visited and drank coffee, was the key. I literally carried it grasped tightly in my hand until I returned to my office and collapsed in my chair. My retelling of the story to fellow employees drew condescending and skeptical looks. I think that God did hear my prayers of desperation and that somehow He took care of the problem for me.

One final example of answered prayer that I do not feel can be attributed to chance. My father, age 93, had been in failing health for about a year. I had consistently prayed for his healing and restoration as I loved him very much. One day driving to work after sitting up most of the night with him in a hospital room, I glanced off to the East where the clouds and the rising sun made a beautiful view. I remember thinking, "If I were more of a charismatic Christian, I would believe that God is drawing my attention to Him through this beautiful sky." Almost immediately a conviction settled on my mind that I had been very selfish. Who was I to keep asking God to spare my father? Perhaps it was time for him to depart to the presence of his Heavenly Father. I prayed a brief and unsophisticated prayer, "Lord, have your own way. If you want to have dad depart this life now, your Will be done." I completed the drive to work and went to the routine morning meeting. I had just taken a chair when I was beckoned to the telephone. It was my son, an internist with the hospital where my father lay, telling me that I had better get back as he felt dad was not going to live much longer. I rapidly drove the fifteen miles back, picked up my mother from her home and rushed to the hospital. When we entered the nursing station area, some of the good people at this wonderful hospital came to meet us. Looking beyond, I noticed that the door to the room was closed. While the staff cared for my mother, I entered the room and saw by father's body laying on the bed. He looked totally at peace. My son sat on the edge of his bed while a nurse stood by talking quietly. My son indicated that he had been talking to his grandfather and helped him to turn on his side to make him more comfortable. While he held my father's arm, he died peacefully. What was even more comforting was that my son had also experienced a "feeling" earlier that morning and had also prayed that God's Will be done in my father's destiny. I was further blessed by the kindness and warmth of the hospital staff which confirmed my belief that God is good. How is that for one of those coincidences?

Yes, the Lord is present through the working of the Holy Spirit. He is aware of our every thought, concern, and need. Nothing that happens to us is unimportant in His eyes. Since this is evident from our personal experiences, our observations of nature around us, and from the testimony of Holy Scripture, isn't it strange that we work so hard at not taking more advantage of this holy relationship? Not as it affects us, you understand, but as it relates to the awe and worship that we should sense and offer to Him who created us, redeemed us, prepares us, chastises us, and will one day welcome us into His embrace. Isn't it incredible that if we knew that the President of the United States was in town and might stop by our house, we would be ready and consciously aware of his potential presence every minute and we would prepare to acknowledge him and to honor him (regardless of our partisan politics). However, God, who has blessed us with all riches, is treated like a long absent stranger who we drop a dime on (sorry, it is thirty-five cents now, isn't it?) only when we are in trouble or in need of a favor. Remember, dear reader, God knows our every thought, desire, fear, and sin against Him. We cannot hide from Him nor can we intellectually deny Him. Our greatest fear should be that He might some day say, "I knew you not."

I have a good friend who is an avowed atheist. I pray for him, but I have learned that logic or debate is worthless. In fact, it is often counterproductive. Who can convince someone else of a relationship that is very personal and precious to you, but one that is based upon faith which is provided by the grace of God? Trying to convince a non-believer is like trying to earn your way to heaven by your own merits. It just cannot be done. Whatever you do, don't send your friendly atheist a book on how to believe. He will rip it apart. Recently, one of my sons called and told me that he had invited our friend (the atheist) to a special presentation at a local church by a "former" atheist who had gained some fame and was now on the preaching circuit. My son asked my wife and I to come with them as some sort of friendly moral support. It was a terrible experience. The professed "recovered" atheist pranced, danced, yelled, and bragged. He even worked in a few book plugs. We left the experience spiritually battered and had little in the way of resources to defend when our atheist friend pointed out that he sized the preacher up as a cleaver entrepreneur who had learned he could make more money on the circuit as a preacher than in business as a atheist. I could not argue with his observation. Was this an example of someone who claimed to have found God, rather than God finding him"?

As a brief digression, be careful about who your religious organization invites in for special events. I have attended programs by noted Christian lecturers who warn of the dangers of the Muslim religion, without really knowing much about that faith orientation. I recently attended a service during which a noted religious singing quartet performed. The lead singer gave a testimony on how he had been influenced to perform Christian music by a relative now deceased. He told the unquestioning listeners that this relative still looked down on him from Heaven and encouraged him. When I returned home, I hit the computer immediately, contacting the senior pastor of the church that had sponsored the group, and asked where I might find scriptural support for the claim that our deceased loved ones are watching us from heaven, giving us moral support. His honest response was that he knew of none. Oh well, the group sold some music, gained additional fame, but, unfortunately, were adding to scripture. It did, however make a good story.

So we can like the fact that God through the Holy Spirit is, has been, and will be present. We can also rejoice that true believers still exist in this world who are supernaturally protected from the ravages of Satan and guaranteed in their safekeeping (and what a blessing and support they are to us).

We can also like the fact that God had a plan for each one of us from the foundation of the world. He knew that mankind would fall under the power of Satan. He knew that we could never earn forgiveness for our sin, both original and that which we commit from minute to minute.

He set up a system or a plan that would allow the perfect sacrifice through Jesus providing an avenue for return to Him through belief and obedience. He further realized that we could not believe through our own strength or wisdom, so He gave us the ability to believe and the support to maintain this faith through pure grace. He then made promises to all who believe that there would be a better day coming.

Isn't it so human to reject this simple and free formula and attempt to make everything more difficult? First we accuse God of being cruel since he does not offer salvation to everyone regardless of whether or not they believe in Him. We say, "Certainly He would not allow this good man to perish just because he has a different belief system!" We feel that we can totally ignore God's presence, even to the point that the politicians of this planet attempt to erase any reference to His existence. We superimpose rituals or memberships to which mankind has to subscribe in order to take advantage of God's love. After all, does it really make any difference if communion is taken with wine or with grape juice? Does it make any difference if you are Lutheran, Methodist, Presbyterian, Reformed Church, Baptist, Assembly, or Roman Catholic, if you really believe God's Word and attempt through the support of the Holy Spirit to obey His commands? Does baptism or the Lord's supper save you? Wasn't it really the perfect sacrifice offered once and for all by our Savior? Do God's Shepherds have to wear funny robes or write their correspondence with canned religious lingo? It is the Grace of God acting upon the heart of man through the workings of the Holy Spirit that counts. I think we are going to be surprised when we become conscious of our presence with the Lord when our life on earth is done, to see people that we did not even know were His and, hopefully, not be aware of those who are not with us. The Turnip Truck just reminded me that old ducktail, if he makes it through God's grace, will probably be required to get a more respectful haircut.

When we first released the emergency brake on the old Turnip Truck and removed the rock from in front of the left rear tire, an agreement was reached through implication that we were going to cut to the chase in this book. This promise has not been forgotten. Remember the ideas and thoughts you are about to read are written by a human being who is worthy of salvation only through Grace and not through any wisdom or merit of his own. Skilled theologians might have fancier words, more depth of meaning, and more extensive applications than this old truck driver. However, the reader, by decision to peruse these words, has a turnip patch on his shoulder and a desire for plain words, so let's start loading.

To start with, there are a few basic truths. God does exist. He did, for reasons known only to the Godhead, cause the world and all that is in it to come into existence. He foreknew that mankind would rebel, just as a portion of the angels did before, and that we would all fall under the curse of death. Satan does exist, as does a hoard of his fallen angels. Satan has a goal to destroy God's creation and His relationship to the human race. Before we were ever created, God developed a divine plan to salvage a portion of mankind. Yes, He so loved the world that He sent His beloved Son to live a sinless life and to give Himself as a perfect offering, taking upon Himself all the sin of the world. God raised Jesus from the dead, then sent the third person of the Godhead, the Holy Spirit, to live with and among all who believe in Christ. We do not understand how God chooses who He will select to believe, but we know that He keeps those safely in Christ's protective hands. The Word is preached, those who hear believe by the Grace given by God through the Holy Spirit. Others also hear but do not believe. There is not a basic contradiction here, only a limitation of human understanding. We must focus on the fact that we all deserve condemnation and that it is only through the mercy of God that this great gift of life is given. Yes, the sacrifice was given for all, but not all choose to accept this mystery. If you find this difficult to believe, think about Satan who certainly knows Holy Scripture better than we ever could and who himself walked in the presence of God. How can he justify his continuing rebellion knowing what the ultimate outcome will be? There is a heaven and a hell, both places of eternal existence; one of joy and one of damnation. Your loved ones who die in the Lord are safe. Those who die without the Lord are lost. There is only one way to salvation, and that is through belief in Christ. Good people do not enter heaven on their own merit, no matter how we grieve over their loss. Bad people follow their natural course, many unconcerned about their destiny due to the fog of their unbelief.

Where is Heaven and where is Hell? No one can point to a geographical place in the universe. It is likely a different dimension of existence that we cannot even understand. Remember, we are dealing with the spiritual, not necessarily the physical. Why does God delay in winding up this "human" project? Well, it is true that He would have no one be lost, but I feel that the real answer is that time is also a dimension peculiar to mankind and of a different framework from God's.

We stumble in attempting to understand the concept of the Trinity in our pathetic and miserable absence of knowledge of those things spiritual. At one time I attempted to explain it to myself as the Father and Son in a close relationship and Their power demonstrated through the Holy Spirit. (That is pretty elementary and probably not accurate). I have come to think of the Trinity as three co-equal persons with differential authority or areas of specialization. Three separate and distinct entities in one God-head. Can we explain this further or even begin to understand it? Absolutely not! Is it vital that we understand that? It can't be done. We will understand one day when we stand in His presence, but even then, it is not imperative as the focus will be different. I pray to God the Father in the name of Christ the Son through the power of the Holy Spirit. I suspect that this will do just fine until I am given the Heavenly explanation. Just one word of caution, never dare approach the throne of God without the advocacy of our Savior. We are not worthy on our own. We must be wrapped in the white robes of the ultimate sacrifice of Christ before our presence will even be recognized.

While we are awaiting for our transition here on earth, what are we to do? We are to obey the commands and teachings of Christ, enabled by the Holy Spirit, as much as it is possible. We are to avoid deliberate sin and disobedience. We are to witness to others of God's love for us. We are to study to become wise in scripture. We are to exhort and sustain our brothers and sisters in Christ. We are to be role models to the world, not that this will bring anyone to belief without God's intervention. We must not bring shame and ridicule by our behavior to those chosen by God for eternal life. We are not to forsake assembling together. I do not believe that this necessarily entails membership in some organized religious organization, but we must give and receive strength from those who are likewise saved by Grace. We should not be caught up in the hate and rivalry created by the "wisdom" of men in denominational contradiction. The Turnip Truck runs on straight 30 weight oil. Anything fancier just gums up the works. Hail fellow believers regardless of their interpretations of fine points of tradition. Flee from denominations that teach universal salvation, cultural relativism, or the saving merit of good works. Grieve for those friends and neighbors who cannot, will not, believe. Do not persecute them or bargain with them. That is not your role. Your cleverness is as nothing in comparison to God's grace and power. Become not followers of worldly religious leaders, but give thanks to God for those portions of their talents which are "on loan from God."

To summarize, love God and love your fellow believers. Grieve for the lost and pray that God will call those who do not yet believe.

CHAPTER II
RELATIVES

It is highly doubtful whether there is any other institution in our society that carries as intense emotional content as does the family. It is either the focus of pride or the burden bearer of shame. Rarely does it carry a neutral connotation and at its very mention, it creates an inner charge of energy. The family member who serves as the lightening rod is usually the target of unfathomable praise or indignities. It is a group thing.

We all experience the family. It is well said to be a cultural universal. It is our pride and can be our curse. The building blocks of this entity have changed somewhat over time, or at least we are aware that the structure is different now than we had previously thought possible. It has become more inclusive and perhaps more varied. We now have reconstituted groups, homosexual combines, kinship communes, not to speak of cohabitating relationships that can better be described as "shack-up" situations.

For those of us of a more traditional bent, we all seem to want the idealized structure composed of a strong, yet loving, father and a warm, supportive mother who is the perfect household manager. The perfect father arrives home at night in plenty of time to relax for a brief time with the family before they all adjourn to the dining room for the evening meal. Following dinner the adults gently listen to and support their children as they discuss the opportunities and challenges of the day. The father resolves conflicts, make decisions, and smiles admiringly at his children while the mother basks in the radiance of his approval.

The mother's role is a little more complex than that of her husband. She is always present, even while carrying on a full-time job outside of the home in order to assist with the payment of the bills. She is ever patient, loving, and supportive; balancing the roles of mother, wife, employee, and adult child without a stumble. In addition to all these responsibilities, she cleans the bathrooms. She responds to the public sneers of her "liberated" sisters with a smile of understanding and forgiveness.

We round this picture out with a couple of well-behaved children who appear on the scene to smile and respond to questions with the ever-present, "yes sir" and "yes ma'am." Granted, such a configuration could rapidly become somewhat aggravating and boring to a visitor, but for some of us as parents it remains the "American Dream" and our parental goal.

In reality, this third part of the nuclear family, the children, sometimes fondly referred to as "rug rats" by one of our popular talk show hosts, start out by being nasty, build up some good time during which they appear to be loving to their unsuspecting parents, and then revert again to being despicable. Depending on the persons with whom they choose to link up following adolescence, they may one day become loving again but in a more calculated and contrived manner. All in all, they carry little purpose other than to create havoc and to serve as regenerators of our society. Parents, having been children themselves, can console themselves with the realization that their offspring will too form their own families and will suffer the same torment.

A family's success is largely measured by the perception of outsiders who have not have the slightest idea of what transpires behind closed doors. Frequently, from an external perspective, this little pack of fighting, disruptive, griping little hellions is held up as "family perfect." Sociologists and psychologists love to discuss the nature versus nurture controversy as it impacts the personality and social development of children. There is no doubt from the view of the cab of this truck that children are born bad and "socialization" often makes them worse. Let's get down and dirty here. The mother, with the limited involvement of her husband, produces a bawling, squalling, demanding little "person" who isn't even cute. It always strains one's credulity to observe a female shopper at Wal-Mart, the primary social locale of trade and commerce for folks of all economic strata, lean over another female's shopping cart, look down at the baby who lies drooling and letting off pungent scents which would curdle the stomach of a mule and say, "Oh, isn't he/she beautiful, it looks just like you." The only saving grace is the substitution of "it" for "her/she." The Turnip Truck, even after an unexpected rain on rotting cargo, is often more sensually appealing.

Since this is a book on "how the cow ate the cabbage," rather than a touchy, feely, pabulum view on life, where do I want to take the reader now? Well, the obvious road is to examine what exists rather than what we wish could exist and then to determine how we get to an improved functioning level. It may take super-low gearing from the old rig, but the tires are sound and the transmission oil was up to the full mark, the last time I checked that is. So let's pop the clutch, hammer the shift cane ahead and to the left, and hit the gas.

The family today is too often a pile of smoking debris. The father and mother work their tails off at multiple jobs trying to pay their taxes and still pay their bills. The so-called "quality time" spent with the children is very difficult to come by, for obvious reasons. At one time, when my six children were younger, I worked a full-time job, taught college classes five nights per week, and handled a small private practice on the side. This was not by choice, it was a necessity. I was fortunate in that I had parents who impressed upon me the need to obtain a higher education, which allowed me to enter a labor market which paid the employee a living wage. Many of our folks today work in the service industry, often at minimum wage without much in the way of fringe benefits. A slight detour is necessary here. Do not allow the politicians to convince you that raising the minimum wage is the answer to a family's financial problems. Such a raise, across the board, merely increases the cost of living for everyone. The can of peas now on sale for 65 cents suddenly becomes 85 cents. If the service industry cannot pass along such costs, jobs are lost. Who loses the jobs? Not the management, but the guy or girl who is still in the minimum wage category of employment.

So we have stressed out parents who are working desperately to provide a decent life for their children and some comfort items for themselves. This, in effect, reduces modeling time as well as parental supervision. To give a very basic example of this problem, let us look at the migrant population that is flooding many of our cities and towns. It appears that one of the many factors in the rise of gang activity among third generation immigrants is the lack of parental supervision. Mom and Dad both work long hours, several days per week, while the children either take care of themselves or, through association with other latchkey children, form support groups which may engage in gang activity if subjected to the leadership of a strong individual with anti-social values.

Even if we remove the exceptions, we still have the question of who or what "models" for our children today? Who or what socializes our children into the values and ethics that we wish to establish in their characters? Grandpa and Grandma seemed to have done a better job of modeling. Perhaps they had employment which allowed them to have a higher profile with their children. The wildly spending politicians in our governmental structure were not leeching off so much of their spendable income that they were forced to take on extra employment to support their family and therefore, could spend more time at home with them. This is just a notion that is shared with the truck, me, and hopefully with you.

Then there is the model of all models…the modern day idol in our homes, the television set. Of all the garbage that the old truck would freely haul off, it most certainly would include modern day "entertainment," including situational comedies and other shows which may be differentiated in their intellectual appeal only by the addition of more physical violence. Our idol is worshiped by all members of the family, but especially by the children. It teaches us that there are no absolute rights or wrongs. If something is perceived to be "wrong," it is presented with humor to camouflage its intent. Suddenly it is funny to disrupt marriages, to "shack-up," to fornicate, to commit adultery, or to engage in questionable interpersonal transactions on other levels. Take this little test to check your perception of "Googoo," the name that approximates the intellectual quality of this magnificent idol. Turn up the sound on a situational comedy and then adjourn to another room of your home to listen to the content and message of the dialogue. Listen to the use of the laugh track, indicating that the producers feel that you are too dumb to even know when to laugh at their version of "humor." You see, sometimes we are distracted by the fine appearances of the actors on the programs. We tend to identify with them and to accept them, without being critical of the message that they are parroting. I guarantee you that if you are a person of at least average intelligence and have a concern for your children, Googoo will soon be recognized for what it is, a destructive influence on the morals, values, and traditions of our families. Isn't it strange that Googoo so often portrays our fathers as being bumbling, inadequate, weaklings? Mothers, in turn, are often held up to be nosy old bitties who are constantly trying to disrupt the clever exploits of her children.

When my children were in public high school, we consistently observed a marked change in their attitudes toward family values when each experienced teachers who carried on a crusade to "enlighten" teenagers and guide them into the situational ethics philosophy. This was then reinforced by Googoo in the evenings and by peer groups at activities. Dumb as we were as parents, we thought that our modeling would be an effective counterbalance against such influences. We were wrong and, as parents, we are still paying the price for our naivety. What should we have done? First, we should have had a good old fashioned confrontation with the school teachers in question. Although this may have proven to be useless, such an incident would have served as a marker. Perhaps we should have turned to home schooling, a comment which makes the Old Turnip Truck scrape its brakes. Maybe we should have returned to the parochial school system, with its many limitations. But regardless of these failures on our parental parts, we really needed to have castrated old Googoo. In today's day and age, one cannot merely ban the television set from the home (although such action is tempting). Neither can you count on the good judgment of children or even on the good judgment of parents to be selective in the programming that they choose to view. Perhaps there is a device on the market today, or perhaps there will be in the near future, that will lock out all channels except those that are not focused on brainwashing, destruction of family and personal value systems, or cheap exploitation and thrills. At the time of this writing, it is difficult to suggest networks that are consistently not exploitative, even those which focus on news and commentary. It would be up to the parents to determine the level of toleration that they would have toward political bias in news reporting as well as to the programs that should be allowed in the home. Then the parents must keep a close watch on the other networks that present informational/educational programs which may still have their own hidden agendas. It is so disappointing to tune into a cognitive program on Christianity or on Christ, for example, only to find that the goal of the writers is to challenge the faith of the viewer, rather than to strengthen the historical facts with which they have to work.

The Old Turnip Truck just whispered in my ear, "Stop your agonizing about this issue, you are losing the reader's interest, just place old Googoo behind my rear duals and throw me in reverse…no more issue!" I wish it were so simple. The attempts to force advertisers to influence the quality of programming is likewise of doubtful effect. There are just too many people who do not care about the detrimental effects of entertainment and many who just want more exploitation, savagery, and violence to obtain a voyeuristic fix. Remember, the more you see and hear, the more you are desensitized, and additional trash is needed to meet your expanded tolerance. I often use this example with students: When you hang around with people who consistently use profanity, then pretty soon you will not notice it, and without being aware, you will start to use it as well.

Now we come to the peer group. There is no avoiding its influence on your children, because it is in itself a cultural universal. You tend to hang around people and they tend to influence you. This goes back to the differential association school of thought which suggests that you become what those around you are. You can shelter your children through home schooling or private schools, but even these attempts sooner or later bring your children under the influence of outsiders with their own value systems. This may be artificially minimized by protecting your children until they arrive on the college scene, but then all bets are off. I have taught at the college level on both secular and private school campuses and I find very little difference in the peer group attitudes at either institution. Some of the children raised by "Christian" families are more hellish than those coming from secularly oriented families. You are all familiar with the behavior of many "preacher's kids." These youngsters are often the first to test the family value systems. There is a very simple dual explanation for this phenomenon. First, the term "Christian Family" does not necessarily mean anything about belief systems, values, or morals. It may merely mean that such a family is on a church roll somewhere. It doesn't mean that there is a spiritual access link to the Lord. Secondly, Satan is alive and well, along with his fallen angels. Ripe targets for destruction are pastors, their families, and especially their children. I once heard a sermon to seminarians who were about to leave for Vicarage placements warning them that they now were in the "crosshairs" of the devil and that Satan would have them discredited and destroyed before they permanently entered the vineyard to labor for God's people. The old Turnip Truck would suggest that those young people entering God's work who are not subjected to temptation and chastisement should probably reevaluate their calling. This only makes sense, doesn't it?

What can we do? We can, whenever possible, raise our children in a community of believers. By all means, have them exposed to and involved in a God-fearing church, under the influence of a clergyman who actually believes in the tenants of the Apostle's Creed. This will not totally protect them, but it will paint on one layer of protective sealant. Community may also refer to the physical location of your home. The middle of a city, for example, is not an ideal place to raise a child; however, it is sometimes impossible to avoid. Ideally, your home should be located in an area where there are others of like mind and tradition. This will spare your child some testing and temptation down the road.

Another layer is to make certain that you know with whom your children are associating. Sometimes this takes stringent action and will make you unpopular with your neighbors or acquaintances. I walked out on the lawn one fine afternoon and suggested to a young man who was "flirting" with one of my daughters that he leave and never come back. The sanction for not following this admonition: having his legs blown from under him with my old 12 gauge. This kid carried some serious baggage and the opportunity for a Christian Witness would have taken too long. He got the message and history proved that the correct intervention was taken. Now, of course, I don't suggest this behavior to the reader, who obviously is more civilized and who does not have to drive a temperamental truck, but make certain that your communication is well understood in the defense of your children. There is nothing wrong if your kids are different from those who hang around in the parking lots downtown.

Make certain that your children know that you love them and want the best for them within the Christian paradigm. The parent should not be expected to give unconditional love when it comes to behaviors. You can love your child, but certainly can hate some of his/her behaviors. Your teenage apple of your eye comes skipping up to you and declares: "I am in love with Waldo, I am of consensual age, and we are going to share an apartment next semester at college. We want to find out if we are right for each other." You, in your parental wisdom hoarsely mutter, "Are you kidding, you will not shame this family with such behavior." The little apple, now showing a little ripeness around the core, responds, "I am going to do it, there is nothing you can do to stop it, I will just walk out of this home…and besides, if you loved me unconditionally, you would not be making me feel bad for what I want to do." Sound familiar to some of you? If you have never faced such a situation, you might mutter to yourself, "Sure…I would just drag her by the hair right out of that apartment." Remember, this is someone who can make legal decisions. Instead, all you can do is to make certain that she knows that you love her, but that you do not accept her behavior. The Turnip Truck would also add, "You can return to your home anytime when you are able to admit the error of your behavior and your parents will run to meet you with open arms of acceptance, but do not bring any refuse from the pig pen with you that I will have to load up and haul away later." There will be times when children reaching the magic age of consent must be treated as a stranger or outcast in order to preserve the integrity of the remaining family unit. This is painful, it washes your guts in an acid bath, but pleasant options are not available. During such times, we can only pray to God through our Savior that the Holy Spirit will work on the heart of the outcast to bring him/her to a saving knowledge and faith in Christ. If this is accomplished, all other hurt in the temporal arena pales in comparison. The realtor would chant, "location, location, location." I would substitute, "final destination, final destination, final destination." We are warned that in the last days, family members will turn upon each other. It is happening now, and probably if we were privy to what goes on behind the closed household door, this has been going on for many years. Perhaps it is in God's inscrutable plan that we as parents must suffer temporary temporal pain so that the child might be secured eternally. We cannot and must not question God, instead we must continue to trust and obey.

The sealant can still isn't empty. Be aware of the quality of the interaction with your children. We have already talked about Googoo, our family idol who even takes precedence over a family sitting down at a dinner table together for mutual support and talk. How about the computer? Have you noticed how much time this little machine demands of you? It is a wonderful invention, but sometimes I have to wonder if this is just another blow struck in the effort to destroy family togetherness. "Yes dear, you start supper, I will check our e-mail, and then we can watch television while we eat."

These sabotage efforts aimed at the family can also come from unusual and unexpected directions. Sure, the school demands our children for band practice, football games, and other extracurricular activities. However, it was kind of shocking to listen to a mother who I was seeing in family therapy complain about her church. She said, "I never have a chance to be with my children anymore. When there is not a school function, our church has an activity." You are thinking, "Yes, but the parents can regulate this." Well, unfortunately, sometimes they can, but sometimes they cannot.

The Old Turnip Truck is having its oil changed at this moment in time, so I want to sneak back to a discussion of home schooling, which seems to be sweeping some parts of the country. The reasons given by parents are often the same. They do not want their children exposed to secular beliefs, especially those which question values of family, religion, and traditional institutions. They wish to protect their children and nurture them through love and exposure to God's Word. Now there is nothing wrong with this approach if the following elements are present: a patient loving parent, time, ability, children who will accept the structure and discipline imposed by the parent on a day to day basis, a curriculum which will give the parent guidance, and some sort of base lining or testing which will ensure that the child is keeping up with his/her secular peers in the development of knowledge and analytical thinking abilities. We have all heard the urban legend of the public school teacher telling a parent thinking of entering his/her gifted child into the system, "Don't worry that little Johnny is ahead of other children his age. After a year or two in public school, he will fall back into his chronological level." I have heard variations of this story too many times in too many places to believe that it was really communicated as stated, but it is a factor in considering alternatives to public school placement.

I have a daughter-in-law who is home schooling her three children and is doing an excellent job. However, let us go over the requirements discussed before. She is an extremely patient, loving mother. I don't want to call her a perfect mother, as this might jinx her future family interactions, but she is the type of woman that most children would desire as a mother. She is warm, affectionate, structured, and insistent on proper deportment and behaviors in her youngsters. I will give you an example. When her oldest son was three years old, he pushed against a neighbor walking on the sidewalk in his excitement to catch up with a sibling. Mother called the youngster to her, explained what he had done that was not acceptable, and then went with the child to the neighbor's apartment door to render an apology. Tough love, you bet, but effective, no question about it!

Mother has set aside a room in her basement as a classroom. She has outfitted it with desks, chairs, tables, etc. Classes are scheduled at regular hours and homework assignments are completed on time. It should also be noted that unlike many mothers today, she is not employed outside of the home. This does not mean that she is not an exceptionally busy woman, but the children take precedence.

Her children have been raised since infancy to love and respect their parents and all elders. They tolerated "time-out techniques" which do not work with all children. An admission here, my six would have become energized to buck the system rather than to cooperate. They would have frustrated any mother who would have been given the responsibility of attempting to educate them in the home. Instead of a time-out bench, I would have had to install iron bars on the windows and tavern bouncers on the stairways. In brief, I am saying, that in my humble opinion, not all children are candidates for home schooling no matter how motivated the parent is.

Another factor, which is perhaps a little sensitive, if you are the mother and the educator, make certain that you can comprehend the study materials yourself. High motivation and idealism are not enough if you are personally "educationally challenged." This is not a slap in the face, but a practical consideration. Were I asked to teach my children algebra, I would probably go into night sweats. Oftentimes, mothers share educational duties with other mothers who have certain specialized strengths and, locally, some classes for home schools are taught in a centralized location by a trained teacher. I recently read a letter to the editor in a local newspaper which contained a complaint by a community resident indicating that she was very annoyed by her neighbor's home schooling efforts as the neighbor's children were running up and down the streets "all day long, yelling, screaming, and playing." This is not home schooling.

When one gets into the question of curriculum and standardized testing, I would suggest that you contact a local association of home schooling parents for guidance and advice. It may differ by community or by governmental school authority. If you are new to a community and have difficulty identifying parents who home school, just go to the pastor of a local bible-believing church, and I am certain that you will be guided in the right direction. The Old Turnip Truck would caution you though, as there are some "crazies" out there who are more anti-establishment than they are concerned with the proper schooling of their children. You can usually identify them by their exaggerated smiles, dead eyes, and grandiosity. I should know, my wife once operated a health food store.

Well, the oil change is complete and I hear the old truck rumbling back this way, so I had better get back on topic.

You probably picked up on some negativity in my attitude toward children. My response: you are very perceptive! In today's society one must examine the payoff for having children. Sure, I know it is a hormonal thing at base. But then, there are all other sorts of rationalizations such as the need to carry on the family name, to have someone to care for us when we are elderly (yeah, sure), the love for little helpless replicas, attempts to please the potential grandparents and proof of masculinity (for the potential father, I would hope, of course). Probably the worst excuse that I have heard was, "I want someone to love me." I have spoken to several single women throughout my teaching years who blatantly indicated that they want this little "package of joy," but they did not want a husband. Such an individual would merely be excess baggage in their fantasized interaction with the child who would bring "love" into their lives. Do I hear a valve overheating in the garage?

Along the same train of thought…well, I just did it again, we don't refer to trains in the presence of the old truck…something about turf battles in the past, or something. Anyway, I have long been curious as to why young people "shack-up." These youngsters know that by doing so they are devastating their parents (usually). In discussing this behavior in the classroom setting, one first encounters a great amount of rationalization. "I wanted to get away from an oppressive home."

"I wanted to make sure that he/she was the right one." (The old test drive concept…I wonder if they kick the tires too?) "I felt more secure living with him, after all the campus is dangerous."

"I needed someone to cook, wash clothes, and clean the toilet for me." (Actually I never have heard that one, but I wouldn't be startled to hear it). The most coherent and believable explanation that I have received was from an insightful young lady who was cohabitating: "Our generation is basically selfish. We do not want to be like our parents who have to work so hard and conform to society's standards too strictly. We want to do our thing, have fun, hang loose. We also recognize that so many marriages do not work, so it is merely reasonable to live with someone to check out our relationship and be able to walk away with limited consequences." The old truck just backfired, "She really didn't say that!" Yes she did and I liked her answer. I didn't approve of her philosophy, but I really appreciated her honesty.

Somehow, the "shack-up" philosophy has not seemed to improve the statistical percentages of intact marriages, once the relationship is legitimized, at least in the State's eyes. I still maintain that there are some of us who take our oath of responsibility very seriously, you know the "sickness and health" part. Most of us who have remained monogamous have also grown to kind of like our spouses. They really do become our best friends. We would sooner spend time with them than anyone else around. Old Turnip Truck never was married, so its comments will not be recorded here.

My advice to young men and women: meet, date, court, take your time. If you lose the target, he/she probably would not have been good for you. Take at least a couple of years, regardless of your physiological and psychological desire for him or her. Do not become sexually intimate with him/her prior to marriage. This restraint is good for your character and will save a heap of guilt and explanations should you decide to go separate ways after a few months of dating. Also, if he or she is too quick to jump in the sack, you are probably not his/her first lover. Remember, anyone can pretend to be something they are not for a long period of time. However, it becomes more difficult after a year or so. Guys, look closely at the girl's mother, both physically and behaviorally. Imagine being in your potential mother-in-law's presence for the rest of your temporal life. If your blood runs cold, better look at some other options. Girls, look at the entire family constellation of your special guy's family. If they look like they might be most comfortable grazing around a hay stack under the stars, perhaps some reconsideration might be in order.

Oh yes…there are a few issues that really push the horn on the truck and my sensibilities…the first might be the one-sided unconditional love previously referenced. Closely following this is having your daughter speak these stupid words, "But daddy, I am the only one who understands him." Girls, there are plenty of psychiatrists, psychologists, social workers, prison chaplains, and bartenders who can give him the understanding that he deserves. He is using you, dummy, wake up and smell the roses.

It is extremely difficult for young men and women to meet potential partners in our wild, secular, disjointed society. I read a column in a newspaper years ago, which I cannot attribute fully due to time and faulty memory, but the thought behind it was that one meets the same people in church as they do in a bar, but they move more slowly in the former.

It is easy to advise a young person where not to meet a potential partner. Some of the high risk methods include newspaper advertisements, computer web pages, bars, and street corners. Before we go on to better places, we have to look at a general belief or philosophy that I maintain about finding the right mate. This concept may save you some time reading, as if you totally disagree with what I am saying, just move on to the next subject area. The Old Truck just grinned and muttered, "Yeah, you can be so bold. They already bought the book and with all the mustard and ketchup that the reader has already dripped on it, they can't possibly take it back." Now, as I am not nearly as cynical as the old rig, if the following bothers you, just take a pair of scissors and cut out the offensive material. Don't use a black marker as it tends to leech through the paper, just like the oil spots on the pavement under…well you know who I am talking about.

I have a strong belief in prayer and God's response to prayers which are offered according to His Will. This translates into the conviction that if you are a believer, pray earnestly that His Will concerning a future mate be accomplished and if you are patient, believing that there is a purpose for whatever takes place, you will either meet the right person at the right time or you will be content in whatever transpires. This was a somewhat vague suggestion, so let me try kicking the turnips off the ground and I will make another pass at it. First, what you want in a mate and what God wants in your mate may not be the same. Second, if you do not have a trusting relationship with God, you need not concern yourself with this method. You will probably marry what you deserve. Well, to come back on this comment, some people, regardless of their lifestyles, do not deserve the problems they encounter with a "soul-mate." My apologies to the unbeliever. Now truck, will you get your tire off my toe?

Third, be patient as God's timetable doesn't always mesh with our daily planner. Fourth, be satisfied with the way that you are. This is not about you, but about glorifying God. Some of us were meant to remain single. Look at the old truck…that's right, personification may not be too sensitive here. Can you imagine what the old junker might have met? It is superficial enough to have been attracted by a lot of chrome, in the right places of course. Fifth, look beyond physical beauty. Now don't enter a dating relationship with someone who repulses you, but get to know the person who comes into your life. First impressions often melt when we get to know someone as a person. That large nose may actually become exciting. The truck just whispered, "Think back on those old Studebakers, their grills used to send me!" Sixth, evaluate carefully the friend's attitude toward God. I have met so many individuals who could talk the talk, but were not interested in walking the walk. Just because he or she attends a church does not mean that a belief system is in place. To be unequally yoked can be devastating to a relationship and to a family structure later on. Can he or she discuss a spiritual relationship with meaning? Is it merely a cognitive awareness rather than a spiritual awareness? Scrape off the emotion, that only lasts so long. Go to places where you believe God's people may be present. This does not have to be a church, it could be a restaurant, a secular organization, a college, or even a religious bookstore. Seventh, take a good hard look at what you like doing with a significant other. Do you enjoy just being together or do you need constant entertainment? Do the places that the potential suggests that you go to represent a location that you would like to be when the Lord returns? Can you, hopefully several dates down the turnpike, talk honestly about remaining chaste until marriage, should that be in your future? Does the potential have habits which are offensive? Smoking, drinking, chewing tobacco, picking his/her nose at stoplights, inappropriate scratching…none of those are good signs. Sure they will give up these significant little habits for you, at least for now. Look at the potential's previous friendships and relationships. As believers we are to forgive, but some things would be very difficult to forget. If he or she seems to feel that the only way that you would be interested in a relationship would be to be sexually provocative or spicy in conversation, communicate your concern and determine whether this was merely an aberration. Then finally the last point: pray, pray, pray…and be patient.

Now somewhere back I offered to describe the parameters of a good family. Notice that I do not say, "perfect family," as we have not yet crossed the great divide. My own family, for example, had its pain, its failures, and its heartaches. But it also taught our children's feeble parents to trust in God's Love and His ultimate Will for every soul which we brought into this world. Let's break this down by key word or thought. If I don't do it this way, I will be off and running the dirt roads with the old truck again. You ask, "Why does he refer to dirt roads?" Well, you see there is this little problem concerning annual safety inspections. No highways, no curious troopers looking through their "shades" at the Old Truck's missing windshield sticker.

The family must have headship. This means that Christ must be the Head of the family and the focus of the family must be on God's glory. I believe that responsibility for this headship must be passed on through the male parent. Sure, it is difficult in our society to find "adequate" males who take family responsibility seriously. But ladies, look for one. Anything less will bring pain. When males fail in their leadership responsibilities, the wife has to take over. This is not the way God planned it. Look at the disasters that take place in many organizations under female leadership. The family is just another very complicated organization. Female students jump all over me when comments such as these are made in the classroom, but after a logical discussion, most see my point of view (which is an advantage as I believe it is also God's point of view). Women are more emotional, critical, possessive, and jealous than men. Men do not pick at where another man's hemline falls or how tight the other man's shirt might be. It is part of our hormonal system as men to be a little less intense with others. I believe that this is also why Paul warned that women should be silent in the church and should learn from their husbands. Oh sure, there are clergymen, usually married to overbearing wives, who claim that Paul's comments were only cultural in context. The Old Turnip Truck would backfire at this lame rationalization. Good male leaders in the church are also sometimes difficult to find. Wives, do not undercut your husband with your children. They are not little sounding boards who should listen with rapt attention to the complaints of their mother about the father's failings, either real or imagined. If husband and wife have a problem that cannot be resolved through good communication, they should find a Godly pastor to discuss it with. If you cannot find a Godly pastor and sometimes you cannot, try to locate a believing social worker, psychologist, family counselor, or other professional to help. Often just a believing layperson with whom you have a trusting relationship can help to sort out some of the misunderstandings.

The next keyword is pride. Do not get so caught up with your "perfect" family that you cannot or will not recognize their imperfections. They are not here on earth to be glorified, but to give glory. You are not a perfect father or mother. You are going to fail over and over, but you have a model to emulate as much as is possible. Emulation comes from prayer, obedience, study, and association with other believers.

How does the word "responsibility" strike you? You are responsible for your family and they in turn are responsible to you. Do not have so many children that you do not have time to interact with them. Keep your priorities straight. Throwing money at any problem does not resolve issues. You can work multiple jobs, but if you do not have time to get to know your children, what is the point? I found that six children were no problem when they were small, but ouch…when they entered puberty! Fortunately, I was given, by God, a mate with patience, love, and understanding. She did much better by the children than I could ever attempt to do. I wonder where this genetic predisposition came from? Old truck, did I just hear a wheeze? People wheeze, not trucks!

Next word, finances. It takes money to support a family. Plan ahead, be frugal, and understand that having children is making a trade off with "toys." You will not have the Scion B, if you have thirty-five kids, regardless of your desires. Don't buy your playthings and hope to "make do" with the costs for your family. Sacrifice is necessary. Be man (or woman) enough to understand that a choice was made. You wanted children and now you have them, so take care of them. If you do not ever want children, then men there is a little surgery that you can elect. Don't pass this off on your wife as you are the head of the family and as such your philosophy should be that this is a once around experience. Don't give the lame excuse that you may want to raise children by another woman some day. Such a thought is disrespectful, even in jest.

Live as a family, not as the employer of hired babysitters. Children are a part of you, so let them experience life with you. Go to church together and have them with you in church from the time that they are born. There is no need for this nursery nonsense. They must learn to be respectful of God's House and certainly can be trained to be quiet. Sleeping is good, bribing with candy and Fad-Figure comic books is bad. Come on parents, use the genius that God has given you! When the child reaches the age of accountability and legal responsibility, be prepared to let go. Just as we give "permission" to a loved one to die at a certain point in their life, give the young person the permission to explore life. If you have given them the best you had to offer under God's Grace, your job is done. It is now the youth's role to be responsible or to crash. It is his/her decision. You can pray, feel sorrow, and agonize at what you perceive as failure; it is the youth's time for accountability to God.

Reader, use the thoughts of this chapter for suggestion, comfort, therapy, support; whatever you need. Writing it was the same for me. We all know that we could have done better with our families. We all wish that we could start over again and avoid mistakes. But keep in mind that God is in charge. We are not to question why He allowed certain traumas to enter our family life. We are not to accuse Him of not protecting our children from ungodly influences and individuals. Our role is to constantly praise Him, glorify Him, and hope in Him.

CHAPTER III
RELATIONSHIPS

A distinct shudder went through the old truck as we entered into this subject matter for discussion. It was very much like striking road-kill that had frozen during the night. The truck does not like such experiences at all. It seems to feel that I should be more empathetic. I should understand that I could be running down the road full-bore and stubbing my toe on a frozen armadillo. Keep in mind that full-bore for the truck may imply speeds up to 30 miles per hour.

The truck does not approve for one minute designating our next shared adventure in thought with the ambiguous word, "relationships." What does this mean, snorted the Old Truck? You have talked about religious relationships, family relationships, and now you want to hack away at just plain "relationships"? Yes indeed, I most certainly do. But before I start, I want to digress briefly back to the road-kill. Have you ever wondered why so many macho men carry their hound dogs on the back of pickup trucks? You ride behind these geniuses and watch as their dogs jump from one side of the pickup box to the other, often almost flying over the side. Travel the Texas highways and I will wager that you will spot at least one recently deceased dog that rolled out of a speeding pickup and landed hard without benefit of a parachute. Then comes the finale, car after car striking the poor animal as it lies dazed (but not for long) in the roadway. Can you imagine the highway department employee whose job it is to pick up the fragments, especially after a long hot day in the July sun?

Whose needs are being met here? Are the dogs being entertained by the fresh air striking their noses during their short life spans? Does it make the owner appear more masculine in the eyes of other men as he roars around with his mutts in the back? Is this a conspiracy to protect highway department jobs? I tried placing my daughter's Chow on the back of my pickup one time and spent most of the rest of the day chasing him on foot after he wisely jumped off before he could start his journey to the great beyond.

Ok, alright, I see the motor oil starting to drip on the pavement again. I will get back on subject. It is amazing when a person of my status in life is structured not only by a wife, but by an old truck.

I have a particular interest in relationships, partially due to my clinical background and largely because I am curious about almost everything. I firmly believe that everyone needs some sort of relationship with another human being not only to survive, but to have any sort of happiness. Like it or not, I have a relationship with you, the reader, unless you opened the book at random and it fell open to this page. That doesn't even usually work using the bible to answer spiritual questions.

Our relationship probably has not been totally based on friendship as I fully expect you readers with maternal instincts to disagree with my comments about children. At least I will have some of the women with paternal instincts in my corner. No, I didn't make a typographical mistake, I meant what I said.

If we were working on a scholarly manuscript here, it would be necessary to come up with a definition of "relationship." I am not going to use some expert's opinion, but rather, let's make one up that is meaningful to you, to me, and to the truck. A relationship is merely a connection between two or more individuals that is felt, experienced, recognized, and either valued or despised. It is something that exceeds the usual in trust, can be counted upon, and is not easily violated. Ideally, it is an agape form of love for someone else, which allows us to confide in them, derive energy and comfort from them, and trust them. There now, isn't it better to use one's own short definition, rather than the ramblings of some book writer?

We all have relationships. We all have someone to whom we can turn in order to ventilate emotions, confide fears, seek reassurance, or just feel secure in his/her presence. Years ago, I had a fellow clinical social worker by the name of Chuck with whom I had such a relationship. I would become frustrated, angry, desirous of strangling someone at work. I would then find my way over to Chuck's office where he had a perch on the third floor of a very busy building. I would walk in, close the door, and come unglued. Chuck would look calmly at me, listening patiently, and often would finally smile and say, "Well…!" That was all it took. I had vented my spleen. I knew Chuck would not view me as an inadequate or a terrible person for being angry. He would not use my monologue as a subject for water cooler gossip. And most importantly I felt better. He did not have to say anything comprehensive. With his one word response, although asinine, he was signaling to me that he understood what I was saying and still accepted me, and "loved" me as an imperfect individual, and still "loved" me as a fellow human being. Ok, truck, I realize that we live in a society that is very confused. "Loved" as I use it here is not erotic or sexual, but rather it is accepting and supportive. This will take Chuck off the barbed wire too, if he ever reads this book. Thank you Chuck for having this kind of relationship with me.

I had another friend, Jerry, with whom I also had a relationship. However, Jerry, being a psychologist and also being a very good man, was not as helpful to me when I really experienced frustration because he really was too good of a human being. When I would stomp, slam, and borderline cuss (I try not to do this), Jerry would attempt to explain why the target of my wrath really wasn't so bad. This didn't work. I needed the focus to be bad until I settled down again and became logical in my thinking. Unlike Jerry with his love and understanding for all others, there are some people in the world that I really don't like. There are some people who exist for no obvious purpose (at least to me in one of my rages). I needed Chuck with his smile and "Well…!"

Relationships can be positive, as I have attempted to describe with Chuck and Jerry, but they can also be very influential in a negative manner. For example, I worked with a gentleman years ago who was a very caring, fine individual, except he could not get over the frozen road kill in his path. Someone would treat him badly or would manipulate him for a selfish reason and he would detour politely, not even showing that he was aware of the odor that surrounded such objects on his path. However, he would then go back to his cave and "lay in the bushes," even if it took years to extract justice. I kind of admired this fellow and his ego-defended manner of handling scumbags. When I am hit with such backstabbing, I either react immediately with my mouth working insane babblings, or I internalize the situation and leave with a stomachache. No such problems for my friend. Revenge was a game and he was the chess master. Have you ever been "unjustly" provoked to the point that you heard the message that you were communicating and were aware of your movement toward the offender, with only fate keeping you from squishing the little jerk on the floor? Not good, but I am afraid that it happens to all of us at one time or another. We look back on it with a little shame, but also with a little amusement and pride.

I had the privilege of working under the supervision of another master of revenge. He did not lay in wait nor did he lose his "cool." His psychic handling of the situation was to declare that the offender was now officially "dead." They no longer existed in his environment or awareness. He was very comfortable with his psychological manipulation of his pain. No revenge, no festering anger, no pulling of the scab off the ego; the problem was pronounced resolved and it was so. The old truck just slipped a gear, so it is necessary to clarify: dead did not mean any physical harm to the offender. It merely meant that to my boss, the problem and person no longer existed in his conscious awareness.

I like outspoken, brutally honest people. You never have to try to figure out who they are and what they might be feeling or thinking. Likewise, weasels make me very uncomfortable and that is probably why I have so few really close friends. The truck, my wife, my mother (provided that the latter two are quietly looking out the windows at the passing countryside), my faith, and my thoughts are often all I want or need during rough times.

To survive this transitional part of our life, what do we really need for relationships? First of all, our primary and most important relationship must be with the Triune God. We must have an awareness of the Father's Glory, the Son's Love, and the Holy Spirit's enabling. If this relationship exists and is building through Grace, nothing can pull us down or destroy us. This relationship is difficult to explain to others as it is intensely personal and private. Each individual can only know what his/her relationship is to God. You cannot know the quality or substance of my relationship. You cannot even know what it might be for your spouse, your best friend, or your family members. You can only pray that they too will find such a relationship and come to their own understanding of it. I recently heard a preacher expound on a radio program that unless you come to Christ through belief and faith by the operation of the Holy Spirit, you will not fulfill that relationship of being with God when this journey is complete. This is a frightful thought, but true. This is why so many prayers of believers are focused on asking that God, through Grace, will enable friends and relatives to enter into such a "relationship." You can know that you have a relationship with God if when things start to go badly, you can turn to him in prayer. This may be a superficial relationship on your part, but it is also an indication that you have a realization as to whom your always present "friend" is.

A second level of relationship is with your spouse. It is often said that a spouse must not only be someone you love, but also must be one of your best friends. If this is the case, our definition of relationship might work here. However, you must be cautious and use good common sense in the use of your domestic relationship. Sometimes your spouse may not be an especially good listener. Sometimes there is so much garbage already on the table that more does not need to be piled on at this point in time. Sometimes you may just need to "grow up" and handle some of the problems by yourself.

The old truck just flickered its running lights. It saw a digression approaching and wanted to warn the reader. However, I am already there, and perhaps the flickering was just due to a short in the wiring. Anyway, let's explore growing up in a relationship. One of the big complaints that I hear from young women is that it is very difficult to find a man nowadays who is strong, dependable, and mature. A well-adjusted woman does not want to enter a marriage in which she has to provide the strength, the stability, and the leadership. She wants a man who she can trust when the times get tough. I married a woman who often questions, disagrees, and wants to discuss upcoming decisions. This is ok, as long as someone takes final responsibility and a decision is made. In a good marriage, it is up to the man to take final responsibility for decisions being made, while making sure that he has heeded the input that his wife has given him. "Hey," snort the feminists who have insensitively been given this book for Christmas. "We can make the decisions without a man's involvement." Ladies, this is up to you, it is your choice and decision. I am only going by what I interpret from God's Word. This is good enough for me and I hope that it would be good enough for you. However, to grow up in a relationship is much more difficult. The wife is often more emotionally mature than the husband. If the husband cannot handle the changes in his life brought about by the marriage, he will either overcompensate and want to be the family tyrant, or he will pull back and allow his wife to make all the decisions, which will ultimately frustrate both of them. This is not the substance or groundwork for a good marriage.

Ideally, a marital relationship will bring together two people, separate from in-laws, who will so care for each other that communication will be open and honest. If there is some failure of traction such as when the old truck lifts its rear right tires on hard turns, it is up to the couple to set some quiet time aside to examine problems, look at options, and set realistic solutions. There does not have to be complete conviction on one solution by both partners, but the best option may be selected, and then let life go on. Do not be stalemated by trying to reach the ultimate decision, as it may not be within human possibility. Then, when a decision is reached, do not look back and worry that the incorrect option has been selected. That will merely bring irritation into the relationship.

That horn in the background signals that I am again going to get on topic. To sum it up, your relationship with your spouse can be extremely valuable in facing life's challenges as long as the two of you can openly discuss issues, not be judgmental about each other's motivations, and care for each other so much that when bad decisions are made, love is not dinged. If one of the spouses has a tendency toward paranoia, the whole relationship can become compromised. If there is a new change in events, look at with whom your spouse is talking outside of your marriage. Some in-laws delight in taking the critical fork in the road, rather than the constructive pavement to problem resolution.

This takes us to family relationships. What should they be and where do they become pathological? I need to clarify here that I am not talking about your children, but about your parents with you being considered an "adult" child. First of all, there must be a recognition that your primary responsibility now lies with your spouse. This does not mean that you stop loving your own parents, but rather you acknowledge and accept the fact that you have chosen to spend the rest of your life with your spouse, you are now one with your spouse, and you cannot be divided against yourself. Your marital problems must be handled within the confines of your home and not farmed out to your parents for resolution. The old saying, "You have made your bed, now sleep in it," has a lot of credibility. Hopefully, you live within close proximity to both sets of in-laws so that you and your spouse will be able to make comfortable contact with both families without favoring one over the other. Don't expect either to be rational about such visitation, as you are still their child and the person whom you married will always remain somewhat of a stranger to them. The real test often takes place at the first major holiday. Where do you go? Who do you visit? One solution is to have both sides over to your house. However, there are probably other tentacles of family relationships emanating out from the parents, so you cannot be the sole focus of attention. Again, honest communication goes a long way. If one of the in-laws has unresolved issues, that will have to be his/her problem. For distances, a rotation of holiday visits might work. For immediate proximity, hit both households on the same day. For my grandparents, Christmas and New Years became the focus. The paternal grandparents were gracious enough to have the holiday gathering on New Years, which allowed their married children to visit the spouse's relatives on Christmas. Of course, in all honesty, New Years was also my grandmother's birthday which eased the road to a visitation solution.

If you are going to involve any of the extended family into the decision-making process, do it as a couple in full agreement as to what you are doing. Don't bring your interpretation of what your family member said to the table to compare with what Bert down at the garage thought. That just gets too complicated and will soon result in axle grease dripping on the cement floor. Unfortunately, some extended family members are destructive and your marriage works best at a distance from them. This is sad, because often these people are themselves married to sensitive, caring people who get hurt in the fall out. Sometimes an extended family member is so invasive that the adult child must really struggle to honor him or her. About the only option for the young married spouse is to get out of the way and keep off the road. Any attempts at civility are merely grit for the gears.

There is another side to this discussion and that is when an extended family member honestly works at being supportive but non-intrusive and the adult child or spouse is too threatened to accept such a relationship. Forcing the issue is not an answer. Prayer as an intervention and patience (hoping for maturity and healing) are often the only logical solutions

As the hackneyed expression goes, each case is different and the solutions vary. The rule of thumb is just never to let your duals get mired in the mud. Take the freshly graveled road and avoid any soft spots on the edge.

Now let's turn our attention to relationships with friends. A good friend is a treasure, but is difficult to find and to keep. My wife has a "best friend" who lives approximately one thousand miles distant. I would wager that this has something to do with the quality of the friendship. A good friend keeps confidences and wisely avoids in-depth discussions about her friend's spouse. The good friend is the wall against which the splatters of life can be spun and patiently sticks with you until the mud dries and can be scraped off. A friend is always available, but never shows up on the doorstep uninvited. The good friend loves you in an agape type of style, but also has self-respect. The good friend knows the boundaries and pitfalls of interaction and will never take you over the cliff. The good friend has no axe to grind, no dog in the race.

To summarize, relationships are not automatically established. They must be planted, watered, and nurtured in order to have a harvest of trust (just like turnips). Prioritize your relationships to make certain that the most important is first. This, without further comment, is evident. This relationship must be with the Lord. Your next relationship must be to family. Since, ideally, husband and wife are one, that relationship must be assumed. If it cannot be assumed, there is no relationship according to our previous definition. Family consists of your children and of the extended membership, including kin. This level is often the most painful and frequently causes us to detour from maintaining our priorities. The Old Truck would say, "Start your engine, put yourself into gear, but don't forget to bring the spare parts along."

If all goes wrong around you, if your spouse and children desert you, you can still take solace in your relationship with your God, because He will never fail you or forsake you. He is the meaning of "relationship."

CHAPTER IV

REJECTION

How bitter the experience of rejection! We fear even the thought of it. In discussing dating and courtship with college students, I often listen to otherwise confident young men express their reservations about asking ladies out on dates because they fear the embarrassment of being "turned down." Remember our own experiences in high school and college? In my high school class, there was a beautiful and brilliant young lady who had limited dating opportunities because all of us guys were afraid to ask her out.

This creates a dilemma for young ladies. How do they "signal" to the young man that they are interested in being asked out? One young lady attempted to explain her "technique" in a class discussion. She said that she made herself available for conversation with the "target," showing interest in what he was doing at the time, helping him to understand that she was approachable, and hoping that they could identify common interests. Some of the more cynical males in the class responded with veiled references to "stalking," but could not come up with better suggestions.

A natural follow-up discussion point is the question, "Where do you meet young people of the opposite sex in search of possible long term relationships?" Well, you certainly do not find many young men or women of dating age in the churches. Some churches have singles groups, but unfortunately, I have often heard young men and women refer to them as "meat markets." I would take that term at its worst connotation. How about a bar? Do you want to meet your future spouse in a bar? I would hope not. Not only are many bars patronized by desperate individuals, but some of these individuals may be predisposed to addiction. However, keep in mind, the foregoing statement refers to sleazy establishments, not neighborhood taverns in some cities which are vital links to a particular culture. Taverns in ethnic sections of Milwaukee, for example, are often family gathering spots with few observed behaviors that could be criticized.

Other contact spots would seem to be the college campus, employment locations, and perhaps common interest organizations such as political clubs, volunteer organizations, etc. One would be wise to avoid looking for a long-term relationship in some of the self-help groups such as Alcoholics Anonymous and Narcotics Anonymous. These organizations do a vital and wonderful job, but the participants have other objectives on which they must concentrate before they tackle the dating game.

Now there are a number of individuals, both male and female, who seem to have no difficulty in jump-starting the dating process. (The Old Truck once confided that such a procedure can be rather painful from its past experience.) In such cases, the askee may be flattered and honored to receive such direct attention, but he or she also carries the responsibility to use care and if possible to check the history of the one asking. As the Old Truck just whispered in my ear, "Better have her run a check on the VIN."

I was fortunate in meeting my wife-to-be. Her mother worked in the Child Guidance Clinic at which I was doing my graduate placement. She knew a number of young ladies who "needed" to meet this vulnerable, single male and decided to introduce me to her daughter whose mission was to acquaint me with these unsuspecting women. What a mistake for my future mother-in-law! When I met her daughter, the show was over. Miss America could have walked in at that moment and started stroking my head and I never would have noticed.

My wife-to-be just did not suspect what kind of trip wire she had just stepped on.

I want to go elsewhere in this chapter, but at the time of writing, the sensitivity to rejection by college age students was on my mind. However, before I yank the steering wheel to a hard right, I have to leave something positive for the young person who might be reading this material. If you are of dating age, which I suggest should be at least age 18, and you are having difficulty meeting "nice" men or women of the opposite sex, be patient. Live your life, do not become a hermit, learn how to get along with your fellow students or workers, but most importantly pray that God will bring the right person into your life. He will, if you trust and if it is in His plan for you. It may be that some of us are better off remaining single and serving mankind in our vocational or service roles. Little do we know in our loneliness how much pain that we might have been spared having not been in a married state.

Ok, yank the steering wheel, using the spinner that my father always referred to as a "knuckle-buster." We have to get this chapter going in the right direction. The focus: to share opinions on persons, circumstances, and situations that we, as believers, should reject. Instead of discussing the state of being a "rejectee," let us instead talk about being the "rejector."

To begin with, are there some people whom we should reject? In the use of the concept here, I am not suggesting that we should actively seek people out in order to reject them, but rather to dissociate ourselves from them when we have no desire to initiate a state of interrelationship with them. We all know that the principle of differential association would suggest that we become like those with whom we associate on a routine and close basis.

For the purpose of plunging in, like the splash resulting from the front tire of the Old Truck when it accidentally strikes a pothole filled with water, we will start on the global level and progress and digress to the micro situations. Yes, the Old Truck just confided, "Much better to be splashed with water from a Texas pothole than to attract the attention of a wandering dog!"

What should our rejection "factor" be toward unbelievers in our communities and neighborhoods? We are urged to be a "light" to these people. We are to be role models who might lead them to seek further knowledge of our Lord. We are to pray for them and to "love" them. This is all ok on a cautious and selective basis. If you are secure in your faith, go for it. However, if you are the least bit wobbly in your confidence, beware! It is much easier to be negatively influenced by the people of this world than to be a positive influence. After all, is it more likely for you to remember an off-color joke from a person whose feet are firmly planted in this world or for the unbeliever to remember your favorite verse in scripture? When you are around profane individuals on a regular basis and the Old Truck's jack handle falls on your toe, are you more likely to utter an oath that you have heard used over and again or to thank God for the fact that it was not the jack itself that tipped over on you?

Who is most likely to impress and gain a following among teen peer groups? Is it the guy who witnesses about the grace of his Lord or the hotshot who gains attention for his guile and his reckless actions? It is interesting to note that college age girls often readily admit to me that they do want to find a nice young man whom they can depend upon, but they also want him to be a little bad! I would interpret this to mean that nice guys should not be too nice, else they would be too boring.

The Old Truck just snorted, "Make the point!" What I am saying is that hanging out with people of dissimilar beliefs can lead to disaster. The popular of this world are often not those whose focus is on God, but rather on themselves.

Should we reject those who are not believers? Yes, when it comes to how they may diminish or distort our belief system. If you are thinking of marrying a nonbeliever, don't do it. If you can influence your children to "hang out" with youngsters whose faith is being nurtured by believing families, choose to do this. Yes, perhaps they will be disappointed because they are not being included in the "popular" groups, but you are making a sacrifice for your faith and taking such a step will make them stronger for it. Better to "reject" those who would alienate you and your family from your religious inheritance, than to reach out in love and unconditional acceptance which may or may not achieve a righteous purpose. We will never be able to isolate ourselves from "them," but neither should we allow ourselves to become one with "them."

My wife is a Master Reading Specialist, which is basically a title for a teacher who loves to help children and adults learn to read and, more importantly, understand what it is that they are reading. She has expressed concern about some of the popular children's books and their influence on the developing young minds. For example, are witches cute and cuddly? Are evil spirits just playthings for the mind which "everyone knows" don't really exist? Does torrid romance really have to be "imagined" before puberty? Certainly there are good Christian books for young people, but are they made into movies or are they hyped in other mass media outlets? It is disappointing that so many well-intentioned, believing parents minimize the influence such biased and worldly literature has on their children. Sure, you can tell your children that it is all a fairy tale, but is that enough? Think of the literature that you may have read as a child and the lasting influence such literary images left on your mind. I must have read and re-read all of Al Avery's books as a youngster, thrilling to the stories of pilots during the Second World War. (Sorry, Old Truck, your mechanical type was not as glamorous!) I also think of Lloyd C. Douglas and his books that not only impacted me spiritually, but had my talents been different, would have led me into a different professional vocation. As someone has coined about the secular writings, "garbage in, garbage out!" To claim that "we are what we read," is a bit of an exaggeration, but any media input leaves something hanging in our very being. Ok, Ok, the statement was "we are what we eat," but I still like the phrase.

Books which lionize the occult and in turn reduce our sensitivity to thoughts not of God, should be rejected whenever possible. Your children will have to mentally ingest enough falsehood during their educational careers that they do not need it reinforced at an early age at home. No, Old Truck, it is not necessary to burn books or to picket the booksellers who sell trash. Let the people of the world read what they will, but Christian, reject it for your loved ones.

The Old Truck just rolled around to the rear of the shed, so I can sneak in one quick deviation. Do not miss out on the opportunity to read good, age-appropriate literature to children, whether they be your own or those from outside of your family who show an interest. I observe with great satisfaction, even joy, when I watch my wife taking time to individually read stories to my grandchildren. To see the nine year old sitting close to his grandmother, laughing with her at the story content, and to see him reach over and give her a big, unsolicited hug at the end…this brings tears to the eyes of even this old cynical codger. Think how much nicer the Old Truck would have been if someone had read "Texas Highways" to it.

God has chosen whom He has promised to keep safe in the Lord's sheepfold. Let Him take the leadership, and in turn, you should be ready and able to witness to other's of His Love when the circumstances are correct. You are to be used by God at his bidding and in His way. Trying to win others to the Lord by being "Mr. Popular" or "Mrs. Neighborhood Teddy Bear" bypasses the process. This carries a warning to pastors also. Do not be all things to all people in an effort to establish a successful organization. You may be a tremendous speaker, you may have "talent on loan from God," you may have the funniest opening stories, you may be a charismatic personality; but if the organization focuses on you rather than on the glorification of God, you will have a lot to explain someday. To become inclusive of nonbelievers at the expense of scriptural truth will lead only in one direction. I have often wondered whether there should be a dual approach in some churches. One approach would be geared to attracting non-believers who are exploring options while the second approach would be to promote growth and knowledge in the one true faith. You can have your line-dances at the first, if you must; but give the believer already in the fold "meat and potatoes!"

I want to spend a little more time on "church building." I am certain that unless you have a "comfort" church, you occasionally experience some dissatisfaction with what seems to be a trend in the past few years. You want to worship with a group of people, all of whom are giving glory to God and praising His Greatness. However, there is this financial thing. To run an organization takes money, sometimes big money. Sometimes church leaders decide to go into a "canned" program in their efforts to bring in new members and to raise the budget income. To do this, it is sometimes required that the church reach out in non-traditional ways in order to attract new people. Now keep in mind the population from which you are attempting to recruit. Some folks are looking because they have become frustrated with their present church for various reasons. Perhaps it is as simple as not being able to tolerate the pastor. Perhaps it is wanting to escape a stuffy liturgy or, the opposite side of the sacred coin, that of feeling uncomfortable in a church service that has turned into a circus with the pastor being the top-hatted, long-tailed ring master. You know the routine, the bellowing "Good Morning" introduction to the holding hands special at the end of the service. Interspersed are jivey tunes and funny stories. Some people are looking for a church to further business contacts or even socialization. Then there is the small, significant segment of individuals who are truly seeking a closer walk with God and an authentic gathering together with believers. The problem seems to be that the church often has to give up much of its close adherence to doctrine in order to attract and to hold new members. When the newness of baptism disappears, when the new member no longer feels special, when he or she recognizes portions of the observance that do not feel good, he or she will likely disappear, leaving only a name on a church roll.

As each church loses its identity and becomes more of a meeting hall gathering place for a diverse population, many of whom have different understandings of their obedience to God and their responsibilities to each other, new excitement must be mainlined into the system and new entertainment choreographed.

My sincere recommendation to the struggling church is to return to your roots. Develop an identity based upon the traditions of your founders as developed through their study of God's Word. Stop the silly greetings and treat the church (both as seen in its members and in its structure) with respect, as if you were entering to worship a present Lord. Strange that such a statement must be made in our society when it should be clearly understood. Reject change unless it is based upon the Word of God. Reject the idea that many of the commands made to us by New Testament Writers were merely the reflection of ancient cultures and not applicable to modern times. Reject fancy pastors who become more important than the message they are supposed to be carrying. Reject music ministers who wiggle and croon. In other words, put your priorities back in order. If you want a nightclub act, spend your money there rather than dropping it in a church money box marked "Here's Entertainment!"

I am sure that many who read this ask the question, "What is this guy, a separatist who ultimately wants to end up in a Monastery?" No, I don't want to separate from fellow believers, I just want all of us to be authentic. I do feel that it would be really nice to delete the chaff and toss out the tares, but that is not for us to do. What is important is that we do not become the chaff and tares due to our association with others who are not His. Oh, another thing, I would urge some of you to do some in-depth research about what the monasteries really accomplished in past centuries. You will find that some of them maintained the true teachings of God, while living in an evil world with a tainted religious system. I doubt, however, that the Old Truck would like to be parked in a mountainside parking lot outside of an old monastery, as it has some altitude (in addition to attitude) problems.

CHAPTER V

RESIDUAL

Some sights really turn us on. My thing is watching the old truck exercise its hydraulics. It groans, then flexes one side slightly like a muscle builder would tease his spectators. Then the other side cracks and the entire box slowly starts to lift up. Enormous power is being generated while the truck stares straight ahead proudly as if to say, "This is what it is all about!"

We promised right from the get-go that the Turnip Truck would stop here. No political correctness, no simpering in the hope of gaining favor, no convoluted messages. Everything would be dumped on the ground and the rear duals would complete the processing activity. We have traveled together in these few pages through a philosophical discourse, which the truck and I hope will be a framework for the reader in making his/her own decisions in life. However, we would have merely been a passing flash on the highway (oh, sure), if we did not address some issues one by one and give you our combined thinking on them. Now, we do not expect you to agree with all of our comments, but we are certain that you will be intellectually honest in your evaluation of them. We suggest that you "cherry-pick" the concepts that are helpful to you in cutting your way through the fog generated by the institutions and intellectual leaders in our society. We are going to go to a "garage maintenance manual" style, identifying social problems and taking a little time to poke them with the tire bat. Keep in mind that a social problem is something that causes concern for a significant number of individuals in our society. When this chapter is completed, I am going to swing up into the cab of the Old Truck, slam the door until it latches, and then you will be on your own. Since it has been the style of the Truck to offend every reader in at least one observation, we will say our good-byes now and following the final paragraph, you will just have the oil smoke of the truck to keep you company, along with the book, of course.

ABORTION

Who knows the desperation of the woman who as a victim of rape or incest finds herself pregnant? How would we react if we did not have objective distance in which to make our decisions? I believe that most, if not all, believing Christians recognize that the taking of an innocent life is wrong. Now you might argue technicalities as to when the tissue becomes a human being. I personally believe that God knows us from the womb. I do not accept the notion that we are merely animals reproducing our species. Therefore, I believe that we are of God's creation from the moment of conception. I am not going to be able to prove nor even successfully convince someone who disagrees with me. I just know what I believe and what I feel that others living under God's Grace should accept. If you do not really believe in a literal God who is in control of His creation or if you believe that God placed the universe in motion and then retired to His recliner, then what I think really will not matter anyway.

Apparently over 50% of our U.S. population don't care one way or another. Perhaps some feel that this is really a protection of women's rights and an effective means of birth control. I really don't know of any creator or ruler who feels just fine with having members of His creation kill off a large segment of others known to Him and hopefully belonging to Him.

I further would suggest that the reason so many individuals are not horrified at even the more ghoulish aspects of abortion, such as partial-birth abortion, is that the mass media and our politicians are afraid to take on some of the militant women's groups who function under a spirit of delusion.

If you are a believer and attend a religious organization that refuses to take a stand on the evil of unrestrained abortion, it is time to scrape the mud off your shoes and look for individuals who are more in tune with God's Love. This is one issue that you cannot straddle the fence on. It will be uncomfortable when you do take a stand and you will be surprised at the number of your friends who will be on the other side of the road thinking that you are some sort of throwback.

What do we say about those raped or the victims of incest? This is where the oil pan hits the rut. If the female victim is a believer, she will have to make a decision on what she feels is God's Will for her. This cannot be based merely on a "feeling," but a conviction after long hours of prayer and consultation with other believers. No one, not even the most Godly pastor, can make this decision for her. She has to make this decision jointly with the Lord. Hopefully, she will find it, through God's grace, to maintain the pregnancy, and will be sustained by the prayers and support of God's chosen people. If the female victim is a non-believer, she will have to make a decision based on her own value system. We cannot by force cause her to keep a pregnancy that she does not want, but we can educate her as to options other than arbitrary death and convenience.

Oh, sure, you will hear the argument that it is better to have legalized abortions rather than dangerous "back-alley" abortions. Actually the procedure either way is not too safe for the fetus. Where were the people making these complaints when law enforcement was not closing down such operations? Where were the state licensing boards when members of their organizations were active in illegal activities? Were the professionals altruists, trying to spare the psyches of defenseless women, or were these the "big baby" doctors and their kind making the big bucks to avoid awkwardness for someone who was not yet ready to settle down with a infant?

We must be steadfast in the protection of innocent life. We must make certain that our governmental representatives vote to preserve innocent life. We must pray that God will forgive us as a people for allowing this evil among us. We must not however, confront violence with further hate and violence. Such confrontation must be through our governmental representatives in all three branches, through our educational efforts, and through the support of others of us who are of like mind. Ask that your pastor preach at least one sermon against abortion each year. Be very aware of your church's stand on abortion.

Recently in the small town in which I work, members of a church angrily complained when pro-life marchers held up signs of protest against abortion since they had unwittingly placed themselves in proximity to that structure. The signs were not indicating anything about the church. The purpose was community education. However, this church, as relayed through members, wanted nothing to do with organizations which opposed abortion. I hope that others in the membership of that church are in closer harmony with God's teachings than they are with the message of political correctness.

When you learn which advertisers support and promote abortion, write them a letter and stop purchasing their products. Let your friends know so that they might do the same. We need as many believers on their knees as we need those who are in activist organizations. Strange as it might sound, it is sometimes more difficult to be constant in prayer than it is to stand on a sidewalk with a sign.

The Old Truck just nudged me and rightly so. In most pregnancies there are two partners. What about the male participant's responsibility and rights in abortion? First of all, you are going to have the irresponsible young men who disappear into the night. Men who claim that it is the woman's responsibility to avoid pregnancy. Men who claim that they cannot become involved because their primary relationship is with another woman. Men who desire termination of a pregnancy because having the child might compromise their careers or reputations. This level of immaturity and irresponsibility is despicable. Such a man is not a "man"!

Secondly, you have some situations in which the supportive husband merely feels that economically the family cannot afford another mouth to feed. Well, fellow, you should have thought about that in advance. There are some fairly routine surgeries that could have prevented this situation. Now that your wife is pregnant, you are just going to have to find a way to step up to the plate. If no other options are available, there is always the avenue of adoptive placement.

What I am saying is that the man has the same responsibility to bear the decision making process as does the mother-to-be of their child. Godly fathers will have guidance. Hopefully both father and mother are already praying together. Parents who do not know the Will of our Creator will have less of a spiritual burden, but an equal psychological burden in confronting the new challenge. Such fathers may not have the same "maternal" instincts but will be strongly impacted by the gravity of the situation. If they are not, their presence will not linger long in the relationship anyway unless the mother is highly adapted to a "victim" status.

On an equally sensitive note, what about the father of the fetus, whether legitimized in the relationship or not, who does not want the mother to abort their child contrary to the latter's desire? This is tough! It is like discovering a seal leak in the Old Truck. You really do not want to think of such situations. Laws may differ as to such parental rights and probably will change over and over again. From a strictly common sense perspective, however, the father must pray, discuss, check legal remedies, and then accept the final decision that is made. Violence and threat have negative value. The man who is not in a committed relationship must recognize a red flag when he sees one. The married man must first solidify his relationship with God, then seek to heal an obviously nonfunctioning relationship with his wife. After that, he must pray for the forgiveness that is promised to all of us, if we truly repent.

A message young men and young women: these are the kinds of discussions and decisions that you must make before you enter into a relationship, whether it be recognized by the state or the consequence of anomie.

HOMOSEXUALITY

To state that homosexuality is not natural is an insensitive understatement. It is the sort of thing that the ostrich would mutter just before it stuck its head in the sand. Understand it or not, there have been homosexuals as members of the human race throughout recorded history. Like it or not, individuals with these different life-styles have not always been the subject of ridicule or condemnation by the societies in which they lived. In our modern American society, estimates vary according to the "experts," but one can see figures of anywhere from 10% to 20% of our population as not being heterosexual. This does not mean that such a large estimate is accurate, and it certainly does not mean that those counted are practicing their homosexual lifestyles. However, no matter how you look at it, alternate lifestyles must be classified as social problems, if for no other reason than roughly half of our society considers it to either be a problem or is made uncomfortable by its existence.

Most of us have mental images of what Sodom and Gomorrah must have been like. For those of us who were fed upon the historical accounts of the bible, a conviction was deeply embedded in us that God did not take kindly to acts which by definition were not natural according to His creative plan. However, for balance, we must also look at the whys, the how comes, and the variances in such individuals. Just as the portrayal of the mentally ill person is violently skewed in our perceptions, the behavior of many homosexuals is likewise distorted. We need to look at some of the elements which make up our perceptions at this point in time, with the beginning premise that homosexual practice is not acceptable to God just like other sins that are practiced by a rebellious human species are not.

To begin with, homosexual behavior is not the same as effeminacy in men or masculinity in women. Often, gay men are very masculine and lesbian women are strikingly feminine. There are mysteries about each recognized functioning pattern, but here we are speaking strictly about men who are sexually attracted to men and not to women except in the cases of bisexuality, and about women who are "turned on" by other women as opposed to being drawn to men. This being stated, I do not believe that individuals are socialized into homosexuality. If this does happen, I would suggest that there are other predisposing factors. The old construct of a dominating mother and an ineffectual father "causing" the child to be fearful or repelled by his/her own sex, just doesn't track in a consistent manner. If this were a clear pattern, we would have a huge population of gay fellows who had been raised by single mothers. Male modeling is extremely important, but I feel is not a decisive, stand-alone factor.

Then there is the research about homosexuals having different brain physiology or size than heterosexuals. This is an interesting theory which has attached ethical dilemmas. It wouldn't seem very fair to have individuals "robotized" into having an irresistible sexual desire for members of their own sex. (For future reference remember the modifying words "irresistible" and "robotized"). You may also hear the chicken or the egg argument. If a person chooses and pursues a certain thought, behavior, or style, is it possible that the brain physiologically adapts to the different patterns of thought? Admittedly, this is like suggesting that the Old Truck started out as a shiny Reo and then converted into a 1941 International. To cut to the chase, I have not found a good explanation of what causes some people to adopt "abnormal" lifestyles. It is actually less important for the purposes of this discussion to understand the "why," than it is to examine the avoidance of consequences or negative sanctions.

I believe that we are all born into this world as sinners and that we can do nothing on our own to remove ourselves from this category. We are all born with original sin and then begin to develop our own storehouse of offenses as soon as we come to an awareness of what is "right" and what is "wrong." This awareness is further muddied by differential association, economic survival, and our culture. Hopefully, if one has a fairly stable home life and comes under the socialization of good parents and other meaningful members of a support system, an "adequate" conscience is formed. I still like Freud's framework of the Id, Ego, and Superego when trying to formulate our thought process. I do not believe that everyone is born with and perpetually possesses a sensitive conscience that guides one into the socially acceptable manner of behavior.

So, this "adequate" conscience is exposed to pushes and pulls from external and internal sources, which give us an opportunity to choose how we will react. On the highest level, I believe that we can all choose to disobey God's commands or commit ourselves to His Grace. I also believe that this freedom to choose and the selection of options is under God's plan for us and is a result of His Grace. How this works is a divine mystery which we, as foolish humans, cannot even start to fathom. God selects those who He would have be saved. This is not a capricious act, as we all deserve damnation. It is only by His Love that He extends the offer to come to salvation through Christ to those He would rescue and save.

Using this framework, we would have to say that we can break humanity into two segments: those that have found God through Christ and are encouraged by the Holy Spirit, and those who do not know God or do not have God as their priority in life. Unfortunately, this is a good segment of the "religious" population, those who attend church but do not have a saving relationship to their Creator. Making application to homosexuality, those who are of the family of God will be enabled by the Holy Spirit to refrain from homosexual practice. Certainly there will be daily struggles and possibly even discouraging defeats, but the individual repents and trusts. If this is too academic, I challenge you good Christian men to deny that you ever have a lustful thought about a woman who was not your wife. Likewise, is there anyone of us who has not irrationally "hated" another believer, even though we are commanded to love? For the believing Christian whose primary sin is that of homosexuality, he must trust in his God, be nurtured by fellow Christians, and must attempt to restrain himself from continued sinful practice. Will the gay or lesbian, through his or her own strength, be totally capable of avoiding temptation? Absolutely not! This is what this life is all about, struggling through with the reinforcement of the Holy Spirit to live a life pleasing and acceptable to God. We may be "Saints" when we accept Christ as our Savior, but we are bombarded and barraged by the demons of Satan, and we will not be able to overcome until we are wrapped in the White Robes which have been washed in the blood of the Lamb. Isn't it interesting, the closer we attempt to follow in our Master's footsteps, the more we stumble and fall. Have you ever been in a church service, listening to an inspired message, when all at once a foul thought crosses your mind? What do you do at a time like that other than push it out of your awareness and ask for forgiveness that you would ever have something so terrible enter your mind?

The homosexual must decide whom he or she will follow and then embark on the struggle to obey. As fellow believers, we should not condemn, but rather we should support, encourage, and assist in any way that we can.

Now, in our opinion (the Truck and mine), the opposite is true if the homosexual rejects Christ. If this is the case we should separate ourselves from him or her. This means not doing anything that would legitimize the behavior or give the message that such a lifestyle is perfectly ok. Our mass media portrays characters playing homosexual parts as humorous, appealing to our sympathy and implying that they are the object of cruelty by heterosexuals. We should not view such programs and definitely should not support their advertisers. We must teach our children that homosexual behavior is not merely an alternative lifestyle and we must be on guard that our elected representatives not provide affirmative action programs or extraordinary protections for this class. Our approach to them should be the same as it would be to any other unrepentant sinner who we do not want to imprint our family's lives. We do not attack them or condemn them to the community. The condemnation will be left up to God, if that is His decision. Keep in mind, there is much that we do not understand and we would be worse than foolish to attempt to act as consultants to our Lord. Remember, we are to love the sinner, but not his sin.

As an afterthought, isn't it curious that the mass media, with all of its political and social correctness, still make humorous comments about homosexuals and their behaviors? Joking about a particular group shows disdain and fear. It is not the place of the believer to engage in such satire. This lifestyle carries serious consequences and it is our fellow human beings who are being spiritually challenged by this deviance from the traditional mores of our culture and from the commands of scripture.

POLITICS

The old Truck just warned me that I will not be able to admire his hydraulics any more if I keep using generalized subtitles. It likes specificity, a word that it, of course, cannot spell.

But what is to come of our society, unless we clean up the political leadership that we have experienced over the past several years and which will no doubt continue into the future? How can we survive when our elected officials routinely change their positions as rapidly as a worried mother with a baby suffering from diarrhea changes diapers? Why do we keep re-electing politicians when they flat out lie to us? Where are the noble leaders of character of yesteryear? Did they ever exist or were they figments of some historian's literary imagination?

Bear in mind that I am primarily interested in the small group of believers who are living their transition lives here on earth. I can't worry about the larger group of nonbelievers who are probably psychologically insulated from the corruption that takes place in our government today. Certainly the people of this world may have an ethical code, but the question must be raised as to what such a value system is based upon?

It really does not matter what label you put on a politician. A Democrat today may be a Republican tomorrow, if it means maintaining his or her lifestyle and prestige. My wife and I once embarked upon political activism. This was when we were still babes in the woods. We soon learned that "shoe-leather" workers such as we were soon displaced by "wealthy backers" once the candidate successfully won office. Almost without exception, the office-holder soon loses contact with his roots and begins to think in practical ways such as how to cultivate party support, how to position oneself for reelection, and how to become further admired and influential. I had one fellow activist drop out of a campaign with the comment, "I believe that I can do more good on my knees (in prayer) than working for a candidate." At the time I was upset in losing such a good fellow-worker, but considering what our candidate became as he "matured" as a politician, the guy was right.

What is the role of the believer in politics? Well, first of all, know what the issues are and how the candidates claim they stand on them. This is fairly simple. For example, if one candidate supports partial birth abortion and the other one has not defined his position, you probably should back the undecided one until he flips over the line too. Study the candidates and try to determine what their value system was in the past. It doesn't matter that the fellow is a Methodist, Baptist, or Dutch Reformed. You notice how many candidates for public office are former Sunday School teachers, as if that were some sort of spiritual marker? What matters is whether he is a believer and lives a life in which he is attempting to obey. Join groups that work together for the election of candidates. Perhaps you can find an organization made up of members who have the same vision for our nation as you do. Beware of the candidate who is too smooth in talking about how important his "religious" beliefs are. Some of these show up in churches and fill pews just before elections. Look for the fruit that this candidate has produced in the past. The throw away line, "God bless America," means a lot less on a politician's lips, than the supplication, "God forgive this nation for we have sinned." Do not stay away from the polls, this is your duty to vote as an informed citizen. If you don't know the issues, the candidates, or are voting only for some special self-interest, stay home. Remain constant in prayer for our leaders and for our nation. Regardless of how bad our "rulers" are, they would not be in their respective offices except for the purpose of God.

When groups cry "foul" when ranking cards are distributed by groups which claim to be Christian, do not join with the condemnation. Sometimes these rankings are instructive and helpful. But like in everything else, as a true believer, do not attempt to convince through logic someone not being of like mind about the spiritual qualities of an office seeker. It is a vain and wasteful exercise. Those who do not believe have a different agenda.

RELATIONSHIPS TO NON-BELIEVERS

The Truck and I have a good relationship and usually agree on issues of the heart and soul. It cannot quite understand human feelings, but it is a good observer and has been more loyal to me than I have been to it over the years. I will admit, there were times when the mud-flaps needed to be replaced, and I wanted "Back Off" cartoon figures and it wanted "Max's Power Equipment" logos. I usually won, and he bore the humiliation stoically. However, when it comes to relationships between groups of different spiritual orientation, the truck is much more gregarious than I am. It loves to rub bumpers with some of the more exotic imported trucks, probably sharing stories of long hauls in distant lands. It really doesn't care whether the designer and creator of the other rig was a Buddhist, Muslim, or an Atheist, as long as it has a lot of chrome and a loud air horn. I am much more cautious with whom I mingle, as I am very concerned about the effects of differential association, previously mentioned in this continuing flow of verbiage.

I also realize that I will come to odds with other true believers when it comes to their association with nonbelievers. In fact, just last Sunday I read in a local church bulletin about an opportunity to learn how to befriend members of the Muslim religion. Of course, the concept was aimed at witnessing, conversion, or perhaps proselytizing. My question, does it work that way? Yes, we must spread the gospel throughout the world. There must be preaching and instruction. We must not neglect to gather together as fellow believers for mutual support and strengthening. These things I know, the Truck knows, and you know. However, I think the Triune God has a little more involvement in this process, and we had better watch out so that we do not spill transmission fluid on the garage floor.

To begin at the beginning where I should have started anyway, according to the truck, I fully believe that it is God who draws us to a belief in Him. Without the working of the Holy Spirit, I don't feel that anyone would believe, at least with a saving relationship. I don't feel that charismatic preachers using all sorts of psychological and emotional gimmicks can win one soul to Christ. I detest church services in which you suddenly realize that you are the focus of a carefully planned manipulation. I don't think that flooding an alien culture with our "Christian" ideas will convert the majority of that society. For example, you can certainly sell Japanese cars in our culture, but the importing of Asian religions doesn't absorb nearly as well into our living rooms. Why should it be any different for them? I do believe that if God in the Holy Spirit portion of the Godhead would spread over the foreign land, people would be won to Him regardless of whether the nearest preacher were a thousand miles away preening his ducktail.

We are not the salesmen/saleswomen of God's power. We are merely here to witness to others of His love, to struggle with our own temptations, and to not live a life of embarrassment to our Creator any more than can be controlled through our pathetic efforts.

My wife was once a member of a liturgical church which had a fine day school as one of its programs. It was interesting to watch the lack of support that this school developed and its final demise. Sure, it was an expensive project, and couples without school age children soon forgot how important the Christian school influence can be. But what really killed it, and I heard these comments personally, was that a number of families having school age children did not want their children to attend a school that did not allow them to experience the diversity offered by the secular world. They wanted their children to be ready to enter the world arena by having experienced all the temptations that were available in the public school system. They wanted their children to learn to interact with others of different or of no belief, so that they could be prepared for their future here on earth. Ok, unfair use of words, but don't you think parents would be more concerned about preparing their children to experience their futures in the new heavens and the new earth?

I feel that believers should identify with each other and not with the people of this world. Sure, we have to work with them, come into daily contact with them, and sometimes even marry them; but is there a mutual advantage in these circumstances? Is the believer's faith strengthened or further dulled? Don't give me this turnip patch refuse of saying, "Well, they go to church, so they must be ok for my child to be friends with." Even the Truck would say, "Horse manure," and that is one of its least favorite cargos.

What can you do? You can start by seeking out and associating with other individuals and families who are not ashamed of their Lord. Forget the church labels and the technicalities of church ceremony. When you "uncover" another bible believing, God-fearing, individual, do not invite them to "your" church. Rather, invite them out to breakfast so you can become acquainted and learn to "agape" each other. We have met some wonderful people and have received great blessings from strangers by routinely going out to breakfast on weekend mornings. Sundays are especially interesting as people from diverse denominations often come into contact after their respective church services and need the opportunity to confide in each other, "I am not certain what that preacher was saying today, it had something to do with psychological developments in the field of economics." If you have the same Father, the same Savior, and the same Holy Spirit support system, it is not too tragic if you take communion with wine and they take it with grape juice. (Now if they take it with coffee, you might want to step back and take another look!) You can associate with other believing families socially with your children. You can find alternative entertainment venues to the television set, the movies, and "Sam's Strip Club and Cartoon Gallery." Home schooling families have wonderful opportunities to meet with other "believing" families and to share feelings and needs with those who understand what they are talking about.

Don't go around giving others the impression that you are the "Apple of God's Eye." He may not be as impressed as you think. In your dealings with others be humble, be kind, be patient, and be real. Get rid of the soft, Teflon speech patterns and the fake loving smile. Be yourself, miserable creature that you are, because the rest of us miserable creatures can relate to you better that way.

If you have to live around non-believers, whether they are church-affiliated or not, remain sensitive to what you are giving up in the secular relationship. Are you really beginning to enjoy their off-color jokes? Are you falling into the pattern of always criticizing others behind their backs? Is golf or your fraternal organization taking time away from your spiritual interaction with God? If so, it is time to reassess, time to prioritize, and time to take a look at why you are changing and who your god has become. Could that god have become you? Remember, there will be a number of religious people who will be utterly amazed when God says, "I knew you not!" Don't be one of them. Remember, there are strangers in our midst who may have more heavenly credentials than Joe Smuck, the guy you party with. Don't fail to take time to sit down with this stranger over a good cup of coffee and a cranberry muffin at the Edom Bakery and Grill.

Separate yourself from them. Stop comparing chrome duals, air horns, and new tie down straps with them. Instead, feel the comfort and blessing that association with other true believers can bring to you and to them.

Well, now is the time to reach inside of the cab (the outside lever is broken), open the door, pull myself in and commune with my constant companion, The Old Turnip Truck.

Happy highways to you!